# Promoting Popular Participation in Yemen's 1993 Elections

**National Democratic Institute
for International Affairs**

Library of Congress Cataloging-in-Publication Data

Promoting popular participation in Yemen's 1993 elections.
     p.     cm.
  ISBN  1-880134-23-3 : $8.95
  1. Yemen.  Majlis al-Nuwwāb--Elections, 1993   2. Political
participation--Yemen. 3. Women in politics--Yemen.  4. Election
monitoring--Yemen.  I. National Democratic Institute for
International Affairs.
JQ1825.Y465P76  1994
324.9533'053--dc20                                              94-4307
                                                                   CIP

# Table of Contents

NDI Description, Board and Publications

## Yemen

- International boundary
- ★ National capital
- +++ Railroad
- Road

0   50   100   150 Kilometers
0   50   100   150 Miles

SAUDI ARABIA

As Sulayyil

no defined boundary

OMAN

Abha

Najran

JAZA'IR FARASAN

Jizan

Sa'dah

Ash Sharawrah

Wuday'ah

no defined boundary

Wadi Mathwb

Thamud

Sanaw

Thamarit

Habarut

Sadh

Salalah

Harad

Huth

Hajjah

Al Hazm

Zamakh

Wadi al Jiz

Saywun

Wadi Hadramawt

Al Ghaydah

16

Sanaa

Ma'rib

Safir

Shabwah

Ash Shihr

Ra's Fartak

Sayhut

Al Hudaydah

Dhamar

Harib

Nisab

'Ataq

Al Huwaymi

Al Mukalla

As Sufal

Arabian Sea

Red Sea

Zabid

Al Bayda

Habban

Ibb

Ta'izz

Lawdar

Ahwar

Al 'Irqah

Qaysoh

Hadiboh

'Abd al Kuri (YEMEN)

Socotra (YEMEN)

Beylul

Mocha

At Turbah

Lahij

Shaqra'

The Brothers (YEMEN)

12

ETHIOPIA

Aseb

Perim (YEMEN)

Aden

Gulf of Aden

Caluula

Gees Gwardafuy

DJIBOUTI

Tadjoura

Djibouti

Bender Cassim

Maydh

Hurdiyo

Berbera

SOMALIA

48

52

Boundary representation is not necessarily authoritative.

Base 801667 (544986) 4-91

# Acknowledgments

This report reflects the written contributions and analytical insights of several people. Thomas O. Melia, NDI's Senior Associate for Programs in Democratic Governance, was the principal author and redactor. The first drafts of the most significant portions, Chapters 3 and 4, were written by Melissa A. Estok, a consultant to NDI who played a vital role in shaping and implementing the programs described. Palmer Kiperman, an NDI program assistant, was also instrumental in organizing the program and preparing the appendices to this report. Public Information Director Sue Grabowski edited the text. Douglas Stevenson prepared the manuscript.

In addition, we are grateful to Robert Norris who, along with Ms. Estok, worked in Yemen as a field representative for NDI. Norris and Estok first articulated many of the ideas and analyses contained in the report. The democratic activists and political professionals from several countries who volunteered their time to assist NDI in its program in Yemen are noted in the report. We want to make special note of Krassen Kralev, of the Bulgarian Association for Fair Elections and Civil Rights, who twice during the spring of

1993 spent more than a week in Yemen.   As he has in other countries, Mr. Kralev contributed significantly to the dissemination of practical information about developing democratic institutions.

We would also like to thank U.S. Ambassador to Yemen Arthur Hughes and the professionals in his mission who provided advice and guidance to us.  We gratefully acknowledge the financial support that enabled NDI to undertake the work described in this report.  Funding was provided by the National Endowment for Democracy and the U.S. Agency for International Development.

Most of all, we want to express our admiration to and respect for the many men and women who are contributing to the development of civil society in Yemen.  They are an inspiration to democrats throughout the region.

Kenneth D. Wollack
President, NDI
December 28, 1993

*Chapter 1*

# Introduction

## A. Overview of the Yemeni Transition

On April 27, 1993, the Republic of Yemen successfully conducted historic legislative elections. They marked the culmination of a remarkable three-year process of formal integration by two Yemeni states that had been arch-foes for decades and consistently among the least democratic countries in the world.

South Yemen, a former British colony, was by all accounts the most accommodating Soviet client state in the Arab world for more than two decades. Traditional North Yemen was ruled in the late 1970s and through the 1980s by a military-dominated regime. From the capital city of Sana'a, Lt. Col. Ali Abdullah Saleh governed in tandem with traditional tribal chieftains in a negotiated, decentralized style that was perhaps the very antithesis of South Yemen's Marxist-Leninist centralism. In a unique process, these two very different and antagonistic regimes — with only their undemocratic character and traditional Yemeni culture in common — would find their merger facilitated by an increasingly liberal and inclusive political order.

The history making character of this election process, moreover, resonates well beyond the borders of Yemen. The political liberalization underway in the country has established Yemen as the pacesetter for democratization on the Arabian peninsula — and perhaps in all the Arab world. The elections were organized largely around diverse and competitive political parties, and virtually no impediments existed to their operation. Independent candidates, too, were allowed to compete. Uncensored and outspoken print media flourished in the months leading up to the elections, and international visitors were impressed by the level of pluralism tolerated by both state authorities and the competitors themselves. International commerce and contacts, weakened by the Gulf crisis of 1990-1991, are growing.

Yemen deserves praise as a democratic pioneer in the region. At the same time, it would be inaccurate to conclude that Yemen has developed a fully democratic political culture or a well-informed voting public. Illiteracy remains rampant — 60 percent of men and 90 percent of women cannot read a newspaper — thus diminishing the positive impact of the increasingly free press. The broadcast media remains today, as it did throughout the campaign, thoroughly in the service of the most senior government officials. The two governing parties also enjoyed access to other material advantages that put their smaller rivals at a distinct disadvantage. The senior judiciary enjoys a degree of respect and has established some autonomy from the executive, although it is not immune from political influence.

Discrimination directed against women represents one cause for serious concern. As South Yemen becomes more fully integrated into a country dominated by the people and the institutions of traditionalist North Yemen, the limited guarantees of women's rights that had been secured in the socialist and secular south are eroding. The election law provided that women could be full participants in the process as voters, candidates and election officials. But this inclusiveness represented a precarious achievement for democratic development: only one-fifth as many women participated as men, even as voters; and only two women were elected to the 301-seat National Assembly. Nonetheless, by including women in the political process, Yemen established an important and hopeful precedent in the region.

In the neighboring monarchies of Saudi Arabia and the smaller Gulf states, no elections for public office have ever been held, and the rights of women are severely abridged in every respect. Only Kuwait, also ruled by a royal family, has conducted competitive parliamentary elections, in October 1992. But political parties were not permitted there, and the franchise was restricted to a very small segment of the adult population; women were excluded entirely from Kuwait's 1992 elections, along with most men.

Problems arose in the administration of the Yemeni elections. These shortcomings rendered them less accessible to would-be voters and compromised, for a significant number of Yemenis, the secrecy of the ballot. To the extent that flaws in the law and its administration are attributable to inexperience, one can anticipate improvements in the future. A post-election proposal by President Saleh to limit the tenure of presidents henceforth to two, five-year terms similarly reflects a potential move toward regular alternance in power, even if it follows Saleh's own 17-year reign as chief executive.

At many other levels, too, the reorientation of the political system did not give rise before or after the elections to much change in the personnel who rule the state. Those who had earlier seized power through revolution, coups or other violence, held their posts and maintained their influence as the country passed in the early 1990s into a distinctly more democratic era.

President Saleh's political organization, the People's General Congress (PGC), won 122 of the 301 seats in the National Assembly. The Yemeni Socialist Party (YSP), which had previously governed South Yemen as a totalitarian state, won 54 seats, all from districts in the south. These two organizations had ruled in coalition from the time of unification in 1990 and behaved variously as uneasy allies and rivals throughout the election process. Al-Islah, the polyglot Islamist party that emerged from the ranks of the PGC once pluralism was legalized, won 62 seats. (See Appendix I.)

While the YSP and al-Islah are ideological opposites in many respects, each of them sought partnership with the PGC as the elections unfolded. Following the elections, both parties joined the PGC in forming a consensus-oriented government that commands a vast majority in the legislature. While the Socialist prime minister, Haidar Abu Bakr al-Attas, retained his office, the cabinet was reorganized to introduce some new faces, including five ministers from al-Islah, including First Deputy Prime Minister Abdul-Wahab al-Ainsi. The leader of al-Islah, Sheikh Abdullah Bin Hussain al-Ahmar, was elected speaker of the National Assembly.

In late September, the legislature elected a five-member Presidential Council that in turn selected one of its number as president of the republic. This election of the Council was delayed for several months (constitutionally, it should have occurred within 30 days of the legislative elections) by two issues. First, some Yemenis, including President Saleh, desired that the constitution be amended by parliament to provide for the direct election of the president. But the presentation of constitutional amendments was slowed by the inability to arrive at a formula for direct elections that was acceptable to Vice President Ali Salim al-Bidh and significant elements of the YSP. Second, once it was decided to move ahead with the existing indirect elections of the president and vice president, the strong showing of al-Islah prompted its leaders to insist upon one of the seats in the Presidential Council. (Since unification in May 1990, the PGC had held three seats and the YSP two.) Significantly, President Saleh and the PGC wanted to maintain the tripartite political consensus, and so considerable time and energy was invested in finding a solution. While a permanent settlement of the vice president's concerns has not, at this writing, been found, one of the PGC's seats on the Presidential Council was reassigned to al-Islah.

On September 26, the following men were elected by acclamation in the National Assembly to be members of the Presidential Council: from the People's General Congress, Secretary General Ali Abdullah Saleh, and Deputy Secretary General Abdul Aziz Abdul Ghani; from the Yemen Socialist Party, Secretary General Ali Salim al-Bidh and Salem Saleh; from al-Islah, Vice President Abdul Majeed al-Zindani.

On the following day, the Council selected from among their number the incumbents, Lt. Col. Saleh and al-Bidh, as president and vice president, respectively. However, Vice President al-Bidh was by this time so unhappy about several issues, including unresolved murders of several Socialist Party officials and the concentration of power in the hands of the president, that he boycotted his own investiture as vice president. As 1993 came to a close, the political standoff between north and south had reached crisis proportions.

Yemen has been frequently dismissed as a backwater in the Arab world, lacking oil riches or a cosmopolitan center. Yet in the first half of 1993, its considerable political progress established the country as the most democratically developed and stable Arab state — and as such, worthy of study and emulation. While the Yemeni consensus in support of unity and the process of political liberalization was still intact at year's end, personal and partisan rivalries constantly threatened to unravel the new order. Informal discussions were underway among prominent political figures about a new constitutional framework that would provide for a degree of decentralization within the unified state. The resolution of the present constitutional deliberations will demonstrate whether the direction and pace of democratization in Yemen will be sustained.

## B. NDI's Program in Yemen

Responding to requests from several quarters in Yemen, the National Democratic Institute undertook two major initiatives intended to enhance popular participation in the election process. NDI conducted these projects from January through April 1993.

- NDI provided training and financial assistance to the nonpartisan National Committee for Free Elections, a project of the Yemeni Organization for the Defense of Rights and Liberties. NCFE systematically mobilized more than 4,000 Yemeni volunteers to observe the elections at polling stations throughout the country.

- NDI conducted a detailed assessment of the barriers that hinder women's participation in the political process, as a first step toward the expected development of longer-term programs to help Yemeni women more fully enjoy their rights as citizens. Moreover, NDI utilized the training program for domestic election monitors to demonstrate that women can participate in public affairs more fully than has historically been the case in Yemen.

During the course of implementing these two programs, NDI sponsored three multi-national delegations of political professionals to Yemen and maintained a near-continuous staff presence for the seven weeks leading up to voting day. NDI thus helped indicate to Yemenis, in the political leadership and in the public at large, that the international community supports the movement toward democracy and is prepared to assist as appropriate.

NDI also invited and arranged for three officials of Yemen's Supreme Election Committee to join NDI's international delegation to observe the February 27 presidential election in Senegal. In addition, NDI convened a one-day pollwatcher training seminar in Sana'a for political parties in mid-March. Finally, NDI invited a prominent Yemeni newspaper publisher to join a survey mission to Morocco in late March. That mission analyzed the political environment preceding June 25 parliamentary elections there.

Subsequent to Yemen's election, NDI has invited Yemenis to participate in other programs and will continue to look for opportunities to help them strengthen relationships with democratic activists around the world. In October 1993, a Yemeni civic leader joined a multi-national delegation that monitored the legislative elections in Pakistan. In December, the chairman of the NCFE joined a survey mission to Jordan.

### Chronology of NDI Activities

Two multiparty Yemeni delegations visiting Washington, D.C., in September 1992 requested that NDI and other organizations monitor their country's first multiparty legislative elections, then scheduled for November 22. On November 6, 1992, the elections were abruptly postponed to April 27, 1993. In December, Foreign Minister Abdul Karim al-Eryani visited Washington and expressed to NDI his government's interest in election-related assistance, and specifically in observation missions. (See Appendix II.) NDI responded by organizing a survey mission to Yemen in January. The resulting program represents NDI's first substantial democratic development initiative in the Middle East.

### 1. First Pre-Election Mission

From January 26 to February 2, 1993, NDI organized a multinational pre-election survey mission to Yemen, led by John Bruton, a member of parliament and the leader of Fine Gael, the principal parliamentary opposition party in Ireland. In addition to Bruton, the delegation comprised Krassen Kralev, regional director of the Bulgarian Association for Fair Elections and Civil Rights (BAFECR) in Varna; Thomas O. Melia, NDI senior associate; and Melissa Estok, an advisor to NDI.

The mission's purpose was to assess the political atmosphere in Yemen and specifically to advise NDI whether it should conduct a program in support of the April 27 elections. NDI planned the trip to coincide with a similar exploratory visit jointly organized by the International Foundation for Electoral Systems (IFES), of Washington, D.C., and the Electoral Reform Society (ERS), of London, which was also planned for late January. The NDI delegation met with the IFES-ERS group several times during the stay to ensure coordination.

During its visit, the NDI team interviewed party leaders, government officials, members and staff of the Supreme Election Committee (SEC), human rights activists, jurists, academicians, journalists and others. (See Appendix III.)

Yemenis of every political inclination and tribal affiliation spoke without hesitation and with considerable pride about their country's political liberalization since the 1990 unification. At the same time, the NDI delegation detected a widespread disquiet during this survey mission (confirmed in subsequent visits to Yemen) concerning the integrity of the election process. These sentiments were especially pronounced among adherents of opposition parties and were shared by numerous journalists, academicians and entrepreneurs — and apparently by some portion of that half of the adult population that did not register to vote in January and February.

In order to dispel some of the cynicism about the election process, the NDI team suggested to the SEC, among other recommendations, that it publicize its election preparations to Yemeni political leaders and the public, as well as to the international community in order to increase public confidence in the process. In a January 31 letter to SEC Chairman Abdul Karim al-Arashi, delegation leader John Bruton emphasized the potential calming influence of a domestic observer group and noted that such an initiative would complement the work of international observers. (See Appendix IV.)

At conclusion of this initial survey, NDI decided to provide technical assistance and material support to local Yemeni election monitors. Several factors contributed to this course. On February 1, NDI received a request for assistance from the newly formed National Committee for Free Elections (NCFE). (See Appendix V.) Chaired by Mustapha Noman, the NCFE was a project of the Yemeni

Organization for the Defense of Rights and Liberties, a well-known human rights advocacy group.

In the course of the NDI delegation's meetings, the foreign minister, the SEC chairman and leaders of all the principal political parties had concurred in the view that properly trained domestic Yemeni monitors could make a constructive contribution to the election process. In this light, NDI concluded that the presence of credible Yemeni evaluators of the political process — to expand and inform international observer efforts — would provide an important boost to public confidence in the results of the election, especially on the part of losing parties and candidates and their supporters. Moreover, in NDI's view, the development of civic organizations would contribute to the broader democratization process in Yemen.

A letter from NDI to SEC Chairman al-Arashi was delivered before the delegation departed Yemen on February 2, informing the SEC of NDI's inclination to reply positively to the NCFE request. (See Appendix VI.) On February 5, NDI wrote to Foreign Minister al-Eryani explaining its plans to work with the NCFE in support of the SEC's work. (See Appendix VII.)

IFES and ERS offered to assist the Supreme Election Committee in the material preparation for the voting and in the training of election officials. The International Republican Institute (IRI), which had dispatched a survey team to Yemen in October, announced that, in response to the government's invitation, it would send an international election observation delegation at the time of the April voting.

### 2.  Interim NDI Staff Visit

Thomas Melia returned to Yemen February 20 and 21 in order to discuss organizational procedures and strategies with NCFE leaders. He also met with several government and political party officials to describe NDI's program to support this new group. The SEC's vice chairman informed Melia that the SEC had voted on February 14 to welcome the creation of the NCFE and to cooperate with it and NDI. As explained in the February 18 issue of the SEC's official publication, *The Elections*, the Supreme Election Committee had instructed its legal committee to develop specific regulations to govern the work of non-party domestic observers. (See Appendix VIII.)

Melia also attended a February 20 briefing held by the SEC for the press and the diplomatic corps. According to SEC officials, the briefing was prompted by recommendations made by the January NDI delegation to the SEC to publicize their preparations for the elections more widely. During the briefing, SEC officials reiterated their commitment to a fair, transparent process, as well as their support for the work of domestic observer groups. During the televised briefing, NDI was specifically acknowledged and thanked by the SEC's vice chairman for its work with the National Committee for Free Elections.

### 3.   Second Pre-Election Mission

NDI sponsored a second pre-election international mission to Yemen from March 9 to 16. The program offered guidance to the National Committee for Free Elections on election monitor volunteer recruitment and training, and sponsored training workshops in six cities for Yemenis interested in joining the NCFE in nonpartisan election monitoring. Each member of the international faculty had previously led similar citizen monitoring initiatives in his or her own country. More than 600 Yemenis, including more than 100 women, participated. The six-member team also organized a conference in the capital city for party agents on monitoring polling stations on election day.

Following the training program, which is described more fully in Chapter 3, the delegation met with party leaders, prospective candidates, national and governorate level SEC members and staff, as well as government officials at the national and governorate levels, to assess pre-election preparations and to discuss the role of domestic and international observers.

### 4.   Third Pre-Election Mission

From March 30 to April 6, NDI dispatched a seven-member international delegation specifically to analyze women's participation in the political process. The NDI team conducted three dozen interviews in large cities and small towns during the seven-day period to obtain the views of both women and men across the spectrum of Yemeni political and civic life. Chapter 4 reviews in detail the findings of the delegation.

### 5.  Mission to Senegal

As an extension of its effort to provide Yemenis with information about international standards for free and fair elections, NDI invited SEC Chairman al-Arashi to designate two members of the SEC to join an international delegation organized by NDI to observe the February 21, 1993 presidential election in Senegal. The 38-member delegation comprised legislators, party leaders, election experts and regional specialists from 16 countries. The Yemeni participants included Ahmed Charaf al-Den, secretary general of the SEC and Raqia Homeidan, a member of the SEC. Yahya Mohammed al-Sayaghi, a foreign ministry official who had been seconded to the SEC, accompanied the SEC members.

The Yemeni members of the delegation utilized the opportunity to compare and contrast Senegal's election system with that of Yemen. They subsequently told NDI staff that they had gained a greater appreciation for the inclusive nature of the Yemeni system, in which the political parties named the election supervisory body, while the Ministry of the Interior administered the elections in Senegal. They also left Senegal with increased respect for the role of international election observers and became proponents of such observers in SEC deliberations.

### 6.  Mission to Morocco

From April 11 to 17, NDI conducted a survey mission to Morocco. The delegation was led by Lewis Manilow, chair of the NDI Board of Directors Middle East Committee. The five-member team visited the country two months before national elections scheduled for June 25. NDI invited Hisham Bashraheel, editor in chief of *Al-Ayyam*, a weekly newspaper published in Aden and Sana'a, to participate. The delegation met in Rabat and Casablanca with political party leaders, government officials, union leaders, human rights advocates, intellectuals and women's rights activists.

Bashraheel was able to witness election preparations underway in another Arab state, one that few Yemenis have visited. Bashraheel returned to Yemen to write three major essays for his widely circulated newspaper on political developments in Morocco and the role of the international community in supporting democratization. (See Appendix IX.)

## 7. NDI Presence in Yemen

Following the second pre-election assessment mission, NDI advisor Melissa Estok remained in Yemen until May 1 to continue to work with the NCFE and prepare for a second round of regional training conferences during the week before the April 27 elections. On April 4, Estok was joined by NDI advisor Robert Norris, who also worked full-time during April as an advisor to the NCFE. He and Estok assisted the NCFE in the development of the its work plan, conducted training sessions on volunteer recruitment and offered advice to NCFE leaders regarding the preparation of training manuals for volunteers. Both Estok and Norris met regularly with the SEC, government officials, party leaders, candidates and other Yemenis throughout the duration of their stay in Yemen. They also sought to coordinate with the programs being implemented by IFES and IRI.

## 8. Election-Week International Observers

By election day, the SEC had officially accredited more than 50 international observers, not including journalists. While a complete list is unavailable, 19 observers served on the delegation organized by IRI and three each served on delegations sponsored by the Electoral Reform Society and IFES. NDI deployed three officially registered international observers — Norris and Estok having been rejoined in late April by Melia. The NCFE conducted a briefing for the IRI delegation and provided information to Yemeni and foreign journalists during the week of the elections. Additional details on NCFE activities are provided in Chapter 3.

These NDI-sponsored activities were designed to help Yemenis realize the democratic promise contained in the historic turn to multiparty elections and political pluralism. The development of truly participatory politics and responsive governance requires the presence of a civic culture in which citizens can peaceably organize, express their views and present reasonable demands to the state. While much remains to be done, significant steps toward meaningful democracy have clearly been taken in Yemen.

*Chapter 2*

# Background

## A. Political History Before Unification

Yemen's history can be traced back more than 1,000 years. In the year 893, al-Hadi bin al-Hussein al-Rassi imposed Zaidi rule in the northern highlands of Yemen and became the first ruling imam. Zaidism is a sect of Shi'ite Islam that originated in Iran but eventually took root in the southwest Arabian peninsula. Here, the Zaidis established a hereditary Muslim theocracy that endured for a millennium — surviving several periods of imperial domination by the Ottomans in the north and the British in the south around the port of Aden. Two decades of insurrection in northern Yemen led the weakening Turkish empire to grant autonomy to the Zaidi imams in 1911 — and full independence in 1918.

During the 1950s, North Yemen's traditional isolationism eased when Imam Ahmed initiated ties with the United Arab Republic, then comprising Egypt and Syria. In 1958, Yemen and the United Arab

Republic formed the federated United Arab States, which dissolved three years later.

On September 26, 1962, the imam was deposed in a military coup led by Colonel Abdullah al-Sallal, who established the Yemen Arab Republic (YAR). Civil war broke out between royalist forces, supported by Saudi Arabia, and republicans, aided by Egyptian troops. Fighting continued until 1970, although the republicans steadily gained an upper hand. The republicans prevailed even after the Egyptian military withdrew in 1967, when most of the 40,000 troops were recalled at the time of the Arab-Israeli Six-Day War.

During the 1960s Yemen began to function along somewhat more modern lines, as the republican administration established communication, transportation and educational systems for the first time. Although religious courts continued to enforce *sharia* (Islamic law) in many fields, "republican decrees" issued by the Revolutionary Command Council constituted the law of the land. Coups and assassinations led to a half-dozen changes in leadership and state structures in North Yemen. Gradually, by the mid-1970s, the nation's borders were clarified and the supreme executive authority of the new state was established. Nevertheless, traditional regional and tribal rulers, often as heavily armed as the national government, continued to exercise considerable practical authority over much of North Yemen — as they do today.

Meanwhile, the port of Aden in southern Yemen had been a British Crown colony from the early 19th century, governed as part of the Indian Empire. Numerous treaties with neighboring sultans and imams led to the creation of the South Arabian Federation only in 1963. Upon the sudden departure of the British in late 1967, the Marxist National Liberation Front gained control of the country and declared the People's Republic of Southern Yemen. On the third anniversary of independence, the name of the country was changed to the People's Democratic Republic of Yemen (PDRY). While South Yemen encompassed a somewhat larger land area than North Yemen, North Yemen contained four times the population, as well as the more productive agricultural area. The port of Aden was once the second most active bunkering port in the world, but the closure of the Suez Canal during the 1967 Mid-East war dealt it a devastating blow from which it never fully recovered.

Relations between the YAR and the PDRY were strained from the start. Intermittent fighting along the border, spurred by a wave of refugees from South to North, erupted into open warfare in mid-October 1972. The Arab League negotiated a cease-fire later in the month, establishing an 18-month timetable for unifying the two Yemens. Although a unification constitution was drafted, later to be enacted in 1990, this deadline was never met. The next 18 years were marked by alternating periods of armed conflict, mutual efforts at fomenting insurrection in one another's territories, and recurring negotiations for unification. The war was financed and abetted by Saudi Arabia (and its Western supporters) in the North and the Soviet Union in the South.

During these two decades, both regimes changed leaders only through violence. The most recent instance occurred in January 1986 when PDRY President Ali Nasser Mohammed called a meeting of his political rivals within the governing Socialist Party Politburo. Instead of attending himself, Ali Nasser dispatched his praetorian guard to the site, where its members shot and killed four Politburo members. Civil war broke out as rival elements of the armed forces fought for control. The fighting quickly spread from Aden to other parts of the country. The army, reportedly reacting to reports of massacres by the president's followers, intervened decisively to end the fighting, but not before more than 5,000 people (and perhaps as many as 20,000) were killed. Prime Minister Haidar Abu Bakr al-Attas, who had been in India when the troubles erupted, was named president and was formally recognized by the Soviet Union. Al-Attas formed a new government, and former president Ali Nasser Mohammed, who had fled north, was sentenced to death, *in absentia*, for treason.

In the northern YAR, Lt. Col. Ali Abdullah Saleh assumed power in 1978, after then-President Ahmad ibn Hussein al-Ghashmi was assassinated by a bomb carried by a PDRY envoy. Al-Ghashmi had become chief of state after his predecessor, Lt. Col. Ibrahim Mohammed al-Hamadi, was assassinated in October 1977. In July 1988, the YAR held its first general elections for 128 of the 159 seats of the newly created Consultative Council. Thirty-one seats were filled by presidential appointment. Although political parties were prohibited, more than 1,200 candidates ran for seats. Women were allowed to vote, but they were barred from running for office. Candidates in these elections were obliged to belong to the People's

General Congress (PGC), a loose forum established by Saleh for political discourse and consensus building. Following the elections, the Consultative Council overwhelmingly re-elected Saleh president. These elections were judged by diplomatic observers and many Yemenis to have been reasonably competitive, and they encouraged many Yemenis to believe that the country could hold free, meaningful elections at the national level.

## B. Unification Process

The current political process began with the May 1990 unification agreement, which prompted the liberalization of Yemen and culminated in the April 27, 1993, elections. Although the two states had been committed rhetorically to unification virtually from the time the South secured its independence, ideological differences long kept the regimes at odds. Real movement toward unification began in May of 1988, under the auspices of the YAR/PDRY Yemen Council. This inter-governmental negotiating forum had been established in 1981 during an early effort by the two states to find a *modus vivendi*. But the Yemen Council had remained a hollow formality until it directed the repatriation of refugees following the 1986 civil war in South Yemen. It next oversaw the demilitarization of the border area. Subsequently, a cooperative agreement was reached for developing and producing oil resources in disputed border territories.

In 1989, direct telephone communication between the two Yemens was established and travel restrictions rescinded. During this year, as the Soviet Union was disengaging from its commitments to satellite and client states, the Aden government announced that it intended to proceed with economic and political reforms, moving South Yemen toward a free market system. In December 1989, President Saleh of the YAR and Secretary General al-Bidh of the PDRY's governing Socialist Party signed a draft constitution. The draft constitution called for uniting the two Yemens within one year, contingent upon the constitution winning popular support through a referendum and the approval of the two assemblies.

While South Yemen's political system quickly concurred in the agreement, the plan for unification did not proceed unchallenged in the North. A campaign against the constitution was organized by the Muslim Brotherhood, a banned pan-Islamic fundamentalist movement, which held the constitution sacrilegious because it did not establish the *sharia* as the sole source of legislation. The constitution stated only that *sharia* would be "a principal source" of legislation. Al-Islah ("Reform"), a related religiously oriented political party, also affirmed that the constitution provided inadequate deference to Islam and joined the negative campaign. In spite of this opposition, the constitution was ratified in a referendum in North Yemen on May 15, 1990.

One week later, on May 22, 1990, the YAR and the PDRY officially unified as the Republic of Yemen. The unity agreement called for a 30-month transition period during which time the country would be ruled jointly by the two former ruling parties, the YAR's People's General Congress (PGC) and the PDRY's Yemeni Socialist Party (YSP). The existing total of 18 sub-national administrative units, known as governorates, were retained. The two national assemblies combined to form one 301-seat body, which met in Aden on May 22 to elect a five-member Presidential Council. That Council, on which the North held a three-to-two majority, formally selected Saleh as president and al-Bidh as vice president. Significantly, the South, with only 20 percent of the new republic's approximately 12 million inhabitants, was accorded an equal number of ministerial positions. Indeed, in the merger of two state bureaucracies, political establishments and cabinets, virtually no one lost a job.

In the course of negotiating the details of the unification agreement, the two regimes decided to link the process of unification with democratization. The Joint Committee for a United Political Organization, a body established by the unification agreement, decided to merge the two Yemens into a unitary system. But rather than simply combine the PGC and the YSP, the Committee recommended creating a multiparty system to lead to national legislative elections.

The democratization process included legalizing political parties and permitting an increasingly free press and, consequently, growing public attention to deliberations of the legislature. As envisioned by the Joint Committee, the transition was to culminate in free elections for a new parliament. Once seated, the new National Assembly was to elect a five-member Presidential Council, which in turn would select the president of the republic. Elections for a 301-member

National Assembly were first scheduled for November 22, 1992, exactly 30 months after unification. The elections would be conducted on a one round, single-member district basis, in which a plurality of votes in each constituency would determine the victor. On November 6, the Supreme Election Committee postponed the elections on the grounds that administrative preparations were inadequate. A new date was soon set for April 27, 1993.

*Chapter 3*

# Monitoring the Elections and Promoting Citizen Participation

Elections in countries undergoing a transition to pluralist political systems often take place in an atmosphere of uncertainty, confusion and concern about the ability or willingness of election administrators to organize a fair and impartial process. In many cases, citizens have reason to question the commitment of the incumbent regime — which itself did not come to power through legitimate elections — to guarantee elections free of manipulation. Frequently, it is unclear whether such a government is prepared to relinquish power should it lose competitive elections. Under these circumstances, domestic and international observer groups have assumed an increasingly important role worldwide in promoting free and fair elections.

Well-organized observers — both international and domestic — can play many roles, depending on the circumstances. They can encourage election administrators and contestants to abide by the rules established, to the extent they would be dissuaded from malfeasance by the political costs of exposure. Experienced observers, especially in the pre-election period, can provide information and advice to enable election organizers or contestants to avoid or resolve problems, based on the lessons learned in other countries. They can assure a doubtful voting public, if it is warranted, that the elections are indeed proceeding according to international standards. In many countries, there is a natural temptation for disappointed losing candidates to attribute their defeat to impropriety or tampering during the vote count. Observers can assure them and their supporters that they lost fairly (if, indeed, that was the case). Generally, impartial observers can enhance popular confidence in the integrity of the process and perhaps increase participation. Any or all of these contributions tend to strengthen the legitimacy of governments that emerge from credible elections.

## A. Yemeni National Monitors: The NCFE

As stated in Chapter 1, the January NDI delegation heard a number of doubts expressed about the depth of the government's commitment to free and meaningful elections. Concerns about irregularities included: the manner in which constituency boundaries were drawn; the rumored movement of military voters to affect the outcome of certain elections; duplicate registration; voting with fraudulent identity papers; fear of systematic vote-buying; and improper threats or pressure directed toward voters. Some of the cynicism was likely exaggerated or misplaced. Some of it, however, was potentially significant, at least to the extent that a lack of public confidence in the integrity of the election process could raise questions about the legitimacy of the government that emerged.

In order to promote sounder understanding among Yemenis about international norms for elections, and to contribute to post-election stability, NDI responded positively to a February 1 request for assistance from the National Committee for Free Elections (NCFE).

The NCFE was established by the Yemen Organization for the Defense of Rights and Liberties (YODRL) in January 1993. The

YODRL had been oficially registered in early 1992 and had major branches in Sana'a, Aden and the city of Taiz. Composed of citizens "interested in guaranteeing free and clean elections on April 27, 1993," the Committee planned to analyze the electoral process as a whole and participate in election-day monitoring to ensure its integrity. Committee organizers sought to recruit and train at least one Yemeni for each of the expected 6,500 ballot boxes that would be used on election day.

The chairman of the executive committee was human rights activist and former diplomat Mustapha Noman, scion of a well-known family prominent in Yemen since Ottoman days. His father had twice been prime minister of North Yemen. Other leading members of the Committee included a civil engineer, several lawyers, businessmen, two journalists, a teacher and a physician. They were not all known to one another when the project began, and none (other than Noman) had been previously active in YODRL. But they heard about the early meetings of the NCFE and volunteered to help. The leadership group went through several permutations, as some early activists lost interest while new volunteers appeared. The NCFE hierarchy eventually comprised 16 regional coordinators located in 13 of the 18 governorates, as well as the executive committee residing principally in the capital city of Sana'a.

The NCFE also established an advisory council composed of leading figures from political parties, the diplomatic corps, the medical and business professions, academia and human rights organizations. The council was formed to keep key decision-makers informed of NCFE activities, as well as to underscore the nonpartisan nature of its work throughout the electoral process.

### NCFE Activities

In the eight weeks leading up to election day, the Committee organized two rounds of training conferences for volunteers; developed, printed and distributed written instructions for volunteers and coordinators; mounted a campaign to publicize the existence and goals of the NCFE; and prepared forms to facilitate the systematic collection of information on election day. Finally, the Committee monitored the larger political process during this pre-election period.

NCFE organized its first series of six regional training conferences for volunteers from March 9 to 16, in cooperation with the National Democratic Institute. NDI brought to Yemen Krassen Kralev, regional director of the Bulgarian Association for Fair Elections and Civil Rights (BAFECR) in Varna, who had participated in the January survey mission; Jean Kamau, legal counsel to the Nairobi chapter of the International Federation of Women Lawyers (FIDA) in Kenya; A.K.M. Zaman, field organizer for the Council for the Study of Democracy and Socio-Economic Development in Bangladesh; and Daniella Diaconu, communications director for the Pro-Democracy Association in Romania. All had played leading roles in organizing and training volunteer domestic observers in their own countries. In each of their four situations, as in most cases (including Yemen), the election law was silent on the issue of domestic observers, and suspicion of hidden political motives was a factor. The March conferences addressed the important function of independent domestic observers and the differences between nonpartisan and political party election monitors.

These meetings were held during the Muslim holy month of Ramadan, when virtually all Yemenis fast during daylight hours and daytime activity is significantly curtailed. In 1993, Ramadan began February 20 and ended March 21. Since only a few weeks remained before election day, however, the NCFE and NDI decided it was imperative to initiate a nationwide recruitment and training effort before the end of Ramadan. Despite the rarity of public events during this period, the initial conferences attracted approximately 600 participants in the cities of Sana'a, Aden, Dhamar, Taiz, Hodeida and Hajja. (See Appendix X.)

Throughout the program, beginning with these initial orientation and training sessions, NDI encouraged (and at times insisted on) the inclusion of women in every aspect of the NCFE's work. Two of the four international faculty for the training sessions were women, which illustrated to Yemeni women and men alike that women can play responsible roles in building and defending universal participation in governance.

The presence of women participants at the initial conferences varied greatly among Yemeni cities. In Hodeida, women made up 43 percent of the total attendance, while only 17 percent of attendees were female in Taiz, and 5 percent in Sana'a. No women were present at the sessions in Dhamar and Hajja. Certainly, the greater social conservatism of some regions was an important factor. Yet

NDI staff in Yemen concluded that the small number of women at these and later meetings was not attributable solely to a low level of interest or willingness on the part of women. Rather, the rate of participation by women appeared more often to be a function of the effort, or a lack thereof, made by mainly male organizers to recruit women. It had not occurred to organizers in Hajja, for example, to invite women. None came uninvited. High female attendance in Hodeida stemmed from the efforts of one energetic NCFE member, who called female friends and family members in response to urging by NDI staff. The receptivity of NCFE committee members to NDI's encouragement, and their appreciation for women as an untapped resource, grew as the elections approached. Over time, female participation in NCFE activities consistently increased.

Following the first round of training conferences, NCFE leaders developed written material to be used by volunteers on election day. They adapted manuals and forms that had previously been utilized by Bulgarian, Kenyan, Romanian and Zambian domestic observer organizations. The written material included a statement of purpose, an instruction manual for volunteers, a checklist for observing voting centers and a checklist for monitoring the counting centers. (See Appendix XI.)

The NCFE implemented a second round of regional training conferences in mid-April. NCFE leaders, and NDI in-country representatives Melissa Estok and Robert Norris, conducted training sessions in the cities of Taiz, Mukalla, Aden and Sana'a. During the sessions, participants elected constituency coordinators and reviewed election-day forms for volunteers.

## B. Controversy Over Domestic Monitors

Despite repeated assurances by various party leaders and SEC members that they supported NDI's work with domestic monitors, a controversy arose five weeks before election day. The dispute illustrated the limits to the SEC's autonomy from the government and the president's political organization, the People's General Congress (PGC). The discord also provides a lesson about the state of political pluralism in Yemen in 1993 and the government's hesitation about permitting completely autonomous groups to engage in political activism.

Consistent with NDI's experience in other countries where it has supported independent election monitors, some Yemeni political leaders suspected the NCFE's nonpartisan motives. Accusations circulated that the NCFE was politically aligned with, variously, President Saleh's PGC, the Yemeni Socialist Party, smaller opposition parties, monarchists and so on. Virtually every party, at one time or another, accused the NCFE (and NDI, by association) of being aligned with a rival party. In fact, some of the individuals involved in the NCFE, or the human rights group that sponsored it, had been critical of one or both of the former regimes of North and South Yemen. Some had protested the postponement of the elections, from November to April, and were publicly skeptical about the sincerity of the government's commitment to a meaningful political process. But none of the critics of the NCFE ever provided information to NDI that any of the officials or volunteers associated with NCFE acted in any way prejudicial to the interests of any of the competing parties. In fact, the NCFE's written material, public pronouncements and training sessions emphasized the Committee's nonpartisan efforts.

The successful first round of NCFE/NDI training conferences also coincided with a breakdown in PGC-YSP merger negotiations in mid-March. Apparently, some in the PGC concluded that the NCFE was a YSP-sponsored scheme to denounce and discredit the expected PGC victory in the elections. Whatever their motivation, officials in the PGC (along with some leaders of al-Islah) embarked on a campaign in mid-March to undermine the NCFE. Articles began to appear in PGC papers accusing the NCFE of "well-known" but never stated "partisan connections."

On March 15, the day that the initial series of NDI/NCFE training seminars for pollwatchers concluded, SEC Chairman Abdul Karim al-Arashi announced in a radio address that the SEC would permit only international observers to monitor the elections. This development came as a shock to many organizers and volunteers committed to the concept of Yemeni observers, especially in light of the formal approval that was reported in the SEC's official publication on February 19. Just the day before Chairman al-Arashi's radio address on March 14, the NCFE sent a detailed letter to the SEC explaining the Committee's goals and methods and requesting cooperation with the SEC. (See Appendix XII.) The NCFE leaders wanted to work *with* the SEC, as Vice Chairman Ahmed Othman explained in a statement issued on March 15 immediately upon hearing of al-Arashi's broadcast. (See Appendix XIII.) The NCFE continued to appeal for official recognition, moreover, as al-Arashi had not explicitly ruled out domestic monitors. NCFE leaders also pressed the SEC for a written response to their February 6 request for accreditation. (See Appendix XIV.)

In February and early March, the PGC had refrained from sending representatives to the informal meetings of the NCFE's nascent Advisory Council. Starting in mid-March, however, PGC officials began attending meetings, which frequently included an NDI representative. During these meetings, the PGC representatives demanded that the NCFE reorganize its executive committee to include "genuine independents" of their party's choosing. The principal PGC representative to these meetings repeatedly stated that SEC accreditation was contingent upon the NCFE accepting the PGC designees into leadership positions.

The leaders of the NCFE held lengthy discussions with various party leaders and tried to respond to the expressed perceptions of partisanship. They informed the PGC and other parties that if all of the parties could agree on the nomination of "genuine independents" for the executive committee, they would accept them. The PGC, in conjunction with the al-Islah party, soon produced a list of "independent" nominees that included former government ministers, ex-diplomats and prominent businessmen. All of the other political parties, however, disputed the independence of the nominees, each of whom were said to be a PGC or al-Islah supporter. Yet the PGC and al-Islah persisted with their slate of nominees.

The NCFE thus confronted a dilemma. If the NCFE accepted PGC and al-Islah stalwarts as part of its executive committee, its reputation with other parties would suffer. The NCFE also feared that if it later issued a statement critical of the process, the PGC-designated members might boycott or denounce the NCFE. Yet if the NCFE did not meet PGC demands, the PGC representatives promised to block NCFE certification by the Supreme Election Committee.

The NCFE eventually decided to reject the PGC demands in the interest of preserving its independence, integrity and positive public perception. In the meantime, the NCFE drew up a plan of action to win SEC authorization for domestic monitors and actively lobbied individual SEC members. All Advisory Council members, with the exception of PGC members and allies, affirmed this decision and remained generally supportive of the NCFE.

NCFE members continued to organize, believing that the SEC could be persuaded to reconsider if presented with a well-managed and demonstrably nonpartisan volunteer organization. Efforts were strengthened to ensure that all volunteers acted in a neutral and independent manner. Members of the NCFE executive committee spoke at conferences around the country about the NCFE mandate and the importance of the group's political independence. In the governorate of Hadramawt, an eloquent mid-April appeal for honesty and independence by an executive committee member prompted the voluntary resignation of two local leaders. Both acknowledged that their interest in working for their respective political parties, the PGC and YSP, precluded them from working with the NCFE. Similarly, in the Taiz governorate, district leaders were publicly elected by volunteers at large — with more than 600 volunteers present. Individuals with clear partisan connections were turned away.

## U.S. Congressional Support

Negotiations to regain SEC approval for domestic observers continued on several fronts up to election day. Appeals originated from such diverse sources as Yemeni journalists, political party leaders, university professors, human rights leaders and the Congress of the United States.

In a March 30 letter to President Saleh, Representative Lee Hamilton, chairman of the U.S. House of Representatives Committee on Foreign Affairs, expressed interest in the upcoming elections and support for the work of the NCFE. (See Appendix XV.) On April 2, Senator Daniel Patrick Moynihan, chairman of the Middle East subcommittee of the U.S. Senate Committee on Foreign Relations, and four other senators, sent a similar letter to President Saleh. (See Appendix XVI.) Both letters suggested that President Saleh urge the SEC to consider the importance of domestic observers to secure "the credibility of the fairness of your upcoming elections." The senators exhorted Saleh to "take every appropriate step to ensure that the National Committee for Free Elections is permitted to pursue its activities without hindrance."

On April 6, in a letter to Chairman Hamilton, Foreign Minister al-Eryani responded on behalf of President Saleh. He explained that the SEC had decided that "the outcome of such an experiment would most likely be the creation of controversy and confusion." He said that the SEC considered the presence of political party agents to be sufficient means to safeguard the process. (See Appendix XVII.)

The Supreme Election Committee was created to be an independently run administrative body. The inclusion of nine political parties and two independent members on the panel was presumed to ensure political inclusiveness. The majority of the SEC's decisions were made, by all accounts, on a majority or consensus basis. However, according to some SEC members, the chairman sometimes announced decisions on behalf of the SEC without taking a vote or even soliciting the views of other members. Several SEC members and political activists claimed that the PGC exercised disproportionate influence on the SEC, especially regarding the issue of official accreditation for local observers.

Whereas a majority of the SEC had voted on February 14 to permit domestic observers, no second vote was taken before Chairman al-Arashi announced on March 15 that only international observers would be permittted to enter polling places. Following meetings with other SEC members, NDI advisors Estok and Norris met on April 17 with al-Arashi to discuss the domestic observer controversy. When asked to enumerate reasons for disallowing domestic observer accreditation, al-Arashi simply referred the NDI representatives to an official of the governing party, the PGC, for an explanation.

## C.  Obstacles to the NCFE's Success

The publicity surrounding the SEC decision to deny NCFE domestic observers full accreditation effectively curtailed NCFE development during the month before election day. This notoriety discouraged many volunteers who were generally supportive of the electoral process and hopeful that it would live up to their expectations. It is impossible to estimate the number of volunteers who wanted to work with the NCFE but decided to stay away in the face of so much controversy. NCFE leaders and regional organizers believe that the number was significant. Moreover, from mid-March to April 27, the NCFE Executive Committee spent much of its time negotiating with the SEC and political parties or refuting attacks on the group's integrity. Time remaining to recruit and train volunteers was accordingly limited — and the magnitude of their accomplishment therefore was greater. Most of the 4,200 women and men who formally registered as NCFE volunteers turned out to monitor the process on election day in spite of official discouragement.

### Access to the Media

Limited access to the media posed a second obstacle to the growth of the NCFE. The NCFE was generally denied access to government-owned and -controlled radio and television, which greatly inhibited its ability to disseminate its message. Though there is a prolific, independent print media, most of the newspapers that reported on the activity of the NCFE had limited circulation. In a country with illiteracy incidence approaching 85 percent in certain areas, the broadcast media is vital to raising public awareness. NCFE was unable to reach this market.

The NDI team was generally unsuccessful in its efforts to assist the NCFE in securing fair treatment in the broadcast media. Indeed, NDI's own activities were at times explained incorrectly on television and radio. During several meetings between NDI personnel and government officials, NDI representatives expressed consternation over the decision of the SEC to bar domestic observers. These sessions, however, were inaccurately portrayed on television as emphatic NDI endorsements of the SEC and its success in establishing foolproof mechanisms for free and fair elections. Inevitably, NCFE volunteers around the country expressed confusion and anger to NDI personnel about these televised stories. They demanded to know why NDI was not helping them win official status and was instead seen to be making nothing but complimentary statements about the SEC and the electoral process.

### Yemeni Committee for Free and Democratic Elections

One of the more imaginative and energetic attempts to undermine the domestic observer initiative was manifest in the Yemeni Committee for Free and Democratic Elections (YCFDE). The YCFDE was formed by several journalists and academics in the last days of March to recruit and train domestic election observers. The emergence of the YCFDE was disconcerting though not surprising since a PGC official had previously warned of the imminent formation of a rival group to the NCFE. On March 31, NDI staff shared with YCFDE leaders several publications about NDI projects in other countries that described international practices in democratic institution-building.

NDI conducted two meetings with the YCFDE leadership. During the first session, YCFDE leaders requested both financial support and copies of instruction manuals for election monitors. NDI's representatives encouraged YCFDE members to meet with the NCFE, by then 6 weeks old, to explore strategies for coordination or, at least, a framework for co-existence. The YCFDE never made such an overture and eventually joined the publicity campaign condemning the NCFE's integrity.

The formation of the YCFDE again diverted the NCFE from training efforts in the field. Perhaps more significantly, the rhetorical assaults on the NCFE by YCFDE, as reflected in a statement issued April 24 to the press and international observers, confused some international visitors. (See Appendix XVIII.)

Many of the journalists and election observers present for election day, unaware of the genesis of each group, did not cooperate with either local group. The situation in effect impeded international visitors from engaging in a potentially valuable cooperative effort with independent, indigenous monitors. An April 25 NDI memorandum for international observers tried to clarify NDI's program and its relationship with the NCFE (see Appendix XIX). But this elicited only another tendentious reply by the YCFDE (see Appendix XX).

### The NCFE's Alternate Plan

As election day neared and official accreditation grew more remote, the NCFE leaders developed an alternative plan for their domestic monitoring effort. Since NCFE volunteers were generally assigned to observe the site where each had registered to vote, the volunteers were asked to vote as usual and then simply linger in their respective stations as long as they were permitted. During this time, volunteers were instructed to collect as much information as possible about the process in the individual polling site. While at the polling site, each volunteer was to wear an identification badge designed and distributed by the NCFE.

Since it was expected that most NCFE volunteers would be asked to leave the polling site after voting, the NCFE developed as a back-up plan a questionnaire for volunteers to use to interview voters outside the polling site. The questionnaire asked voters for information regarding the deciding factors in their choice for parliament; their access to information about candidates before the elections; and their opinions about civic groups such as the NCFE. (See Appendix XXI.) Such an exit survey had never before been conducted in Yemen. It provided the thousands of volunteers who had committed themselves to be monitors on election day with a secondary method to gather useful information despite official obstruction of their work.

### NCFE Internal Conflict

As election day drew near NCFE leaders divided their time between organizing appeals for accreditation and conducting regional training conferences to publicize their plans to work on election day with or without official support. As the prospects for last-minute accreditation dimmed, internal conflict surfaced within the NCFE executive committee regarding strategies to respond to the SEC decision.

Two leading committee members suggested a coordinated effort with the YCFDE in order to garner support from the PGC and, eventually, to win accreditation. The majority disagreed, maintaining that a coordinated effort with the YCFDE would compromise the objectivity of the election-day message. Moreover, since accusations of nonpartisanship had been made against virtually all members of the executive committee at some point, the majority contended that a change in leadership would be insufficient to prompt the PGC to support accreditation.

Divisiveness within the NCFE on the issue of accreditation peaked with the arrival from the United States of Ahmed Bahabib. Born in South Yemen, Bahabib is an American citizen who returned to Yemen as an independent election observer on behalf of the Yemen-American Friendship Association, which he founded in 1992 in Virginia. New to the details of the controversy and unaware of its full history, Bahabib was drawn into negotiations with the PGC and eventually offered himself to lead a new umbrella group that would coordinate Yemeni domestic observers.

Based on several meetings with political parties and SEC officials, Bahabib believed that he could obtain accreditation. He persuaded two NCFE members to join him, which led to their ostracism from the NCFE. Bahabib's apparently well-intentioned initiative eventually came to naught and provided an additional source of confusion to international observers one week before the elections. Another unfortunate outcome of this intervention was the alienation of two leading organizers from the rest of the NCFE leadership.

The NCFE proceeded to disseminate its materials to volunteers in the governorates and to distribute daily announcements to the press and international observers starting on April 25. (See Appendix XXII.)

Threats of violence were raised two days before the elections. NDI representatives and NCFE leaders heard from several sources of rumors circulating in government that NCFE volunteers, in the absence of official accreditation, were "planning to force their way into the polling centers" on election day. Government and election officials, and individuals claiming to speak for them, expressed concern that if NCFE volunteers were insistent on remaining in the polling stations on election day, soldiers might retaliate with force.

The NCFE worked diligently to quell these rumors in the final 48 hours before the polls opened. NCFE leaders called their governorate coordinators on election eve to discuss the rumors and to reiterate instructions that volunteers were to raise no arguments and were to avoid any and all confrontations on election day. Any volunteer requested by any local election official or security agent to leave a voting center was to do so immediately. The NCFE also disseminated a special news release on election eve (see Appendix XXIII) and copies of an April 25 letter to the SEC. Both documents sought to assure Yemeni officials, the general public and international visitors that NCFE volunteers would not disrupt the conduct of the elections. During all training conferences and in its instruction manuals, the NCFE had emphasized to volunteers their role "as a camera," recording events but not intruding into the picture.

## D. Election Day

Approximately 4,200 NCFE volunteers were present in 14 of the 18 governorates and in 211 of the 301 constituencies on April 27. NCFE leaders estimate that only 20 percent of the 4,200 were permitted to enter the polling stations and conduct thorough observations during the day. Volunteers carried out much of the observation while waiting in line to vote and while voting inside the polling station. More than 2,000 NCFE volunteers completed reports of varying lengths, most of which constituted a combination of the original checklists designed for inside the polling stations and the alternative described above.

NCFE leaders designed a communication network to receive reports from volunteers by means of telephone calls to and from regional coordinators. Following the receipt of all reports of irregularities, NCFE volunteers were dispatched to the site to confirm the accuracy of the complaint reported. At the end of the counting process, the regional NCFE coordinators carried their written reports to NCFE headquarters in Sana'a where they were consolidated.

Several NCFE volunteers were harassed by party agents or security personnel, and two were ordered arrested in Sana'a in lieu of simply being asked to leave the premises. However, there were no reports of serious conflict or violence prompted by the actions of a NCFE volunteer.

The most frequent election-day complaints received by the NCFE related to questionable procedures practiced by election officials when processing illiterate voters. Part of the difficulty stemmed from the nature of the balloting system; in a country with so many illiterate voters: the voter was given a blank card on which to write the name of his or her preferred candidate. There were many confirmed reports that party agents or election officials incorrectly recorded votes by illiterates. In other cases, the secrecy of the ballot was breached when illiterates were obliged to announce their choice aloud to party agents and election officials. Afterward, the ballots were then marked by an election official and held up for all party agents to confirm that the voter's stated choice had been accurately recorded.

The NCFE also heard widespread reports of local election officials or party agents pressuring voters into voting for a particular candidate. This was especially true in the southern governorates, where the Yemeni Socialist Party won virtually every seat in the territory of the former PDRY. In several districts, government workers and others were threatened with the loss of their jobs or a reduced salary if they did not vote for certain candidates. Threats such as these tend to prevail in an environment where voters do not fully understand the system or where voters fear repercussions from marking a ballot they do not perceive to be secret.

An NCFE leader witnessed one blatant instance of abuse while he waited in line to vote in Taiz. Party agents collected the registration cards of women in line who were party supporters and entered the polling station. There they voted on behalf of the women who were standing outside. The agents then returned the voter registration papers to the women and sent them home.

Ballot secrecy was often compromised, and not exclusively for illiterates. Many voters complained that local election officials instructed them to cast unfolded paper ballots. Due to the proximity of the box to election officials, party agents and other voters, opportunities existed for ballots to be read by those standing nearby.

During the January to February registration period, opposition parties and independent observers charged that the ruling parties had mobilized the military to move units into particular constituencies where the soldiers' votes could influence the outcome of close races. NCFE volunteers consequently anticipated complaints regarding the military on election day. Whether or not the army had been improperly exploited during registration, relatively few such charges arose on election day.

The possibility of double voting also represented a widespread concern before election day. While there were rumors of thousands of extra ballots in circulation, the SEC did not officially respond to these reports. One member of the SEC told NCFE officials that the SEC had contemplated several means to prevent duplicate voting. One solution involved requiring local officials to stamp or sign each ballot as it was handed to the voter. Ballots appearing without the official stamp during the count would be disallowed. Chairman al-Arashi reportedly vetoed such a policy, a move that intensified concerns among opposition parties. Despite considerable pre-election consternation about the probable use of improper ballot cards, NCFE observers heard no such allegations on election day.

In its April 29 post-election statement, the NCFE cited numerous irregularities that violated the spirit and the letter of the law. Some problems originated from the actions of SEC officials at the local level who seemed to have received uneven or inconsistent training.

More often, the incidents were attributed to actions of political party agents. However, the NCFE indicated in its statement that the irregularities of which it was aware had not been of sufficient magnitude to alter the results in any constituency.

Referring to the pre-election period, the NCFE's final statement noted that "the climate of fear and suspicion in many quarters, the minimal participation of women, and the lack of public education about democratic politics rendered these elections less meaningful than they could have been and should have been." (See Appendix XXIV.)

### Interaction Between International and Domestic Observers

As noted in Chapter 1, NDI's work with the NCFE was intended to complement the programs undertaken by the other two Washington-based organizations. IRI was to organize a multinational observer delegation, while IFES was to provide technical assistance to the SEC. Given the Yemeni experience, it is appropriate to describe in general terms the ways in which international and domestic monitors have cooperated in other countries and to explain NDI's rationale for supporting the work of domestic observers.

Relationships between international and local election observer groups differ according to circumstances in each country. At times, the international observer groups treat domestic observer groups as they would any indigenous non-governmental organization. The local observers brief the international delegates on their work and their findings, but the connection is limited to this relatively brief interaction.

On other occasions, international and local groups develop a relationship of closer partnership. Information is continuously shared, and national volunteers and international delegates may be deployed on joint teams. Typically, each group maintains a distinct identity and issues separate statements. NDI has worked on a variety of occasions with domestic groups in this manner.

In a third type of situation, the international observers incorporate local groups into the structure of the international mission. The international group functions as an umbrella under which domestic groups obtain permission to enter polling stations. This arrangement most often occurs when the local authorities are unable or unwilling to accommodate domestic observers.

Each of these arrangements enjoys its own rewards. In every case, international delegates benefit from the knowledge and experience of the local observers. Generally, an international delegation that establishes close links with indigenous nonpartisan groups, as well as with election administrators and political contestants, increases its ability to analyze and to understand the electoral process. Cultural subtleties and relevant history are more likely to be appreciated by the domestic monitors who can interpret events or circumstances for their international counterparts. In cases where observer deployments are coordinated, the international team is able to enlarge its geographical reach by deploying mixed teams to more areas. In exchange for this assistance, local groups benefit from the resources available to most international groups, including enhanced media access. In some cases, a local monitoring organization that did not exist before the elections, or was significantly strengthened during the process, endures as part of a country's civil society long after the international observers have departed.

## E. Conclusions

The National Committee for Free Elections successfully recruited and trained more than 4,200 volunteer men and women, and in so doing became the first nationwide nonpartisan civic organization in Yemen. The original NCFE executive committee was an eclectic group; the majority of the committee members did not know each other before the formation of the organization. Nevertheless, from differing professional and social backgrounds, the members united to work toward the democratic development of Yemen.

The NCFE's training programs helped a large segment of the society understand, and feel part of, the new election process. The visible presence of thousands of independent election monitors and the thorough manner in which they sought to confirm or dispel rumors appear to have contributed to the calm post-election climate.

Finally, the NCFE consolidated information gathered from its volunteers into a report containing recommendations for improving the election process. No such advocacy role was played by any other grassroots Yemeni organization.

**Lessons Learned**

NDI learned a great deal from its experience in Yemen about providing assistance to the democratization process. Among the lessons learned (or confirmed) were the following:

- Some inefficiencies in the work of the NCFE can be attributed to deficiencies in its organizational structure. Inadequate job descriptions and the lack of by-laws constituted the two major problems. Each member of the executive committee held a title that roughly corresponded to his or her duties, but there was no common understanding of what each person's duties entailed or of how each person was related to the others. In addition, there was no precisely defined decision-making mechanism established within the committee.

  NDI's information and advice to the organizers could therefore be improved in this respect, although some recommendations provided to the NCFE on such matters were not addressed. If the internal management of the committee had been stronger, problems such as disputes about how to negotiate with the SEC could have been handled more expeditiously and effectively. On the other hand, the NCFE was explicitly an *ad hoc* initiative destined to last only 10 weeks at most and so it was not unreasonable for those involved to presume that decision-making and coordination could be managed informally. In a stressful environment, however, when unanticipated crises are likely to arise, it is best to have in place an established hierarchy, decision-making process and delineation of duties.

- The program could have been improved had an NDI representative been assigned to work with the NCFE full time in Yemen from January to June. Such a person could have worked with the NCFE to increase its effectiveness by helping establish clearer decision-making processes and definitive job descriptions for executive committee members. The NCFE could have also extended its reach had recruitment efforts begun sooner. It must be noted, however, that NCFE leaders were reluctant to begin recruiting until they received some official standing in the eyes of the SEC. NDI's counsel to the NCFE that it begin development of the organization in order to demonstrate its identity was accepted only slowly.

- NDI was reminded of the importance of clear and effective coordination between domestic monitoring groups and international observers.

## Post-Election Activity

Many of the NCFE leaders and activists have expressed to NDI their desire to continue work in democratic development. They may establish a permanent organization to undertake civic education projects, public polling, monitoring parliamentary activities and observing future elections. NDI is prepared to assist in these efforts.

*Chapter 4*

# Women's Participation in the Political Process

## A. Introduction

Yemeni political leaders, almost universally male, frequently refer with pride to the legal provisions that guarantee women equal access to the political process. Compared to nearby states in the Arabian peninsula, Yemen's political process in 1993 can indeed be characterized as relatively inclusive. For example, Saudi Arabia and most of the Gulf states have never conducted a participatory election. Kuwait has held parliamentary elections, most recently in 1992, although women are not allowed to vote and only a minority of their adult male counterparts possess this right. Numerous facts, however, indicate that the formal equality provided in Yemen's election law is not fully realized in practice.

Very few women occupy leadership positions in Yemen. No women served on the post-unification five-member Presidential Council or were named to ministerial positions. Only a few women currently serve as deputy ministers. Ten women served in the 301-member transitional parliament (established upon the merger of North and South Yemen in 1990), although they were selected in the non-competitive single-party elections conducted in the pre-unification South. The 17-member Supreme Election Committee (SEC), which was created to administer the legislative elections, included only one female member. In addition, only one woman (in the city of Ibb) was named to the three-member supervisory committees established by the SEC in each of the 18 governorates.

Women's participation in the April 27 elections was modest. Less than 500,000 women registered to vote as compared to more than 2 million men. (See Appendix XXV.) This figure suggests that only 16 to 20 percent of eligible women registered. By contrast, an estimated 87 percent of eligible men registered to vote. Only two women won seats; both were elected from areas of the former South Yemen where the Yemeni Socialist Party remains strong.

In general, female candidates were not supported by the principal political parties. On the initial list of registered candidates for parliament (before many candidates withdrew their names), only 44 of the approximately 4,000 candidates were women. The majority of these few women were independents, presenting themselves to the voters without any organizational backing or noteworthy financing. Of the three major parties, the People's General Congress (PGC) nominated two women, the Yemeni Socialist Party (YSP) nominated four women and the al-Islah party nominated none. Interestingly, the traditional Islamist party, al-Islah, organized women to register and to vote more assiduously and more effectively than any other party, while at the same time making clear to their supporters that women ought not present themselves as candidates for office. Indeed, leaders of al-Islah told women voters in public meetings that to vote for women would be "un-Islamic."

## B.  The Survey Mission

In order to understand this aspect of democratic development in Yemen, NDI organized a pre-election assessment to explore the participation of women in Yemen's political process. The mission took place from March 30 to April 7. The specific objectives of the survey mission were: 1) to determine the extent and quality of female involvement in the formal political process; 2) to identify and analyze political and socio-economic factors that impede women's active involvement in the political process; 3) to inquire about indigenous organizations that promote women's inclusion in Yemeni politics and civic life; and 4) to determine the potential for coordination among NDI, the international community and Yemenis in order to enable women to enjoy more fully their rights as citizens. (See Appendix XXVI.)

The assessment mission comprised Farida Rahman, a member of Parliament from Bangladesh; Chilufya Kapwepwe, a member of Parliament from Zambia; Patricia Reilly, a former senior attorney at the Federal Election Commission and deputy legal counsel to the 1992 Clinton-Gore campaign from the United States; Emine Usakgligil, business development manager of the Istanbul Film Agency and former managing director of the *Cumhuriet* newspaper from Turkey; and Yesim Arat, associate professor of political science from Bogazici University in Turkey. Accompanying the delegation were Melissa A. Estok, who had previously visited Yemen twice for NDI, and NDI Program Assistant Palmer Kiperman. Fatima al-Huraibi, assistant to the president of Yemen's Agricultural Cooperative Union, served as interpreter and advisor to the NDI team.

The NDI team spoke with a wide range of individuals and organizations. Those interviewed included: government and election officials; leaders of the People's General Congress (PGC); leaders of the Yemeni Socialist Party (YSP); leaders of several small parties; female independent and political party candidates; members of the Yemen Women's Union; journalists; voter registration committee members; and many female citizens, some of whom had registered to vote and some who had not. The NDI team conducted interviews in the capital of Sana'a, the southern cities of Taiz and Ibb, and the village of Khowlan. (See Appendix XXVII.)

A set of six general questions formed the core of the interview format. (See Appendix XXVIII.) These questions related to women's impressions of the electoral process as a whole; women's participation in the registration process; the extent to which women currently occupy leadership positions and the obstacles to their attainment of such positions; and the impact that the movement toward a multiparty, democratic political system in Yemen would have on women.

The all-female composition of the NDI delegation and the use of a female Yemeni interpreter elicited a frankness and candor by the women interviewed not always manifest with men present. Moreover, three of the international visitors were Muslims from predominantly Muslim countries. Many women remain fully veiled in the presence of men, but with the NDI team they were able to remove their veils to share tea or a meal and speak openly about their experiences. These conditions greatly enhanced personal communication.

Among the sensitive topics discussed were physical and psychological repercussions experienced by women for their participation in the election process, whether as candidates, registration officials or voters; discrimination directed against women in the work place; and the impact on women of the recently enacted Personal Status Law, Presidential Decree No. 20, which outlined terms for family law in unified Yemen. The NDI team was persuaded that many women would have been reluctant to discuss these issues had male colleagues or family members attended the interviews or if men had been members of the international delegation.

The presence of three Muslims on the NDI delegation contributed an understanding and affinity otherwise not possible. They had struggled individually with issues relating to Islamic law in the context of democratizing political systems in their own countries and could share their impressions with Yemeni women. In Bangladesh, for example, a woman has been prime minister since 1991, while another woman is leader of the parliamentary opposition. Moreover, delegation members' experiences with Islamic law lent credibility to the delegation and provided a level of comfort for the Yemeni women to express themselves. The Yemeni women recognized that the delegates had shared similar experiences and were therefore more willing to discuss Islamic law as it is applied in their society.

Yemeni women expressed appreciation for the opportunity to meet and learn from such a wide range of female leaders from abroad. A group of female teachers in the city of Taiz, while offering various perspectives on the situation of women in Yemen, also thoughtfully questioned the international visitors about their lives and status. The answers prompted revealing statements. One of the teachers exclaimed, "It is so good for us to know that we are not alone." She was extremely enthusiastic to spend more time "learning from the experience of women in other countries." It was clear that most Yemeni women enjoy very few opportunities to meet people from other nations.

**Women and the Electoral Process**

The April 27 elections were regarded by all of those interviewed as an important first step toward building accountable, responsive democracy in Yemen. In general, Yemenis were optimistic that democracy would bring about a positive change and that life would improve. When asked to discuss problems, though, several matters arose repeatedly. Women who were interested in the process almost universally believed that a large part of the election results had been pre-determined during negotiations among the principal political parties. In this respect, as in some other ways, women seemed as informed and opinionated as many men.

The women interviewed by the NDI team expressed differing views toward the pre-election negotiations. One woman was comforted by her belief that "the PGC and the YSP are responsible for unification and the election process. There exists some agreement. They will solve problems together." In contrast, another woman referred to the electoral process as "children's play" and argued that "nothing is going to change. The only outcome is that they [political parties] have divided the country." There was also a strong sentiment that districts were drawn and the military was mobilized to favor the ruling parties. These allegations notwithstanding, women expressed pride in the process as an essential learning experience for Yemenis. As one civic leader observed, "People have big hopes for the election. They are ignoring corruption because they believe after the election things will be different."

The election law, which was drafted by a transitional parliament and approved by the Presidential Council on June 8, 1992, stipulates that women have the right to vote and to be candidates. At the initiative of the parliamentary deputies of al-Islah, who persuaded the legislature to amend the election law before final enactment, the SEC was directed to provide separate registration committees and polling sites for women.  Article 5 of the election law states that the SEC "shall take all appropriate measures to encourage women to exercise their voting rights and shall set up women's committees that shall be entrusted with registering the names of female voters..."    As suggested by this excerpt (and many discussions with male and female Yemenis), the premise of this modification was to facilitate the participation of women by segregating them from men.  Otherwise, it was asserted that women would have been reluctant to stand with men in the same registration and voting lines or to have their photographs stored alongside those of men.

Many women maintained that the greatest achievement of the election process was the formal incorporation of women into the election law, even while practical problems remained to inhibit full participation.  The election system provided women with a legal guarantee of equal status that they rarely enjoy in other fields of endeavor.  Before the 1993 elections, women in North Yemen were permitted to vote but not to be candidates.  (Though one woman did register herself as a candidate for the General Assembly in 1988 as a form of protest.)  In South Yemen, women were allowed to run for seats in the legislature, as well as to vote, although voter preference and meaningful choice played no role in these Soviet-style one-party elections.

There was significant concern expressed during interviews that women were not knowledgeable voters.  One factor limiting access to information was the high rate of illiteracy among women.  Official estimates suggest that 85 percent of women are illiterate, compared with 46 percent of men.  Thus, most women are unable to read the growing number of party newspapers that have appeared in recent years, significantly negating much of the potential utility of press freedoms that emerged following unification.

A second factor restricting more political awareness by women relates to informal political debate conducted at meetings where *qat*, a plant chewed for its stimulating effect, is used.  The *qat* session is a daily social ritual in which virtually all Yemeni men participate.  Much of the pre-election discourse took place at afternoon *qat* sessions, from which women are almost universally excluded.  During the gatherings politics is discussed; and a great amount of business, both informal and formal, is conducted.  Though women do chew *qat*, it is not as pervasive a habit as with men; and it is practiced in all-female groups.

### Voter Registration

As previously stated, fewer than 500,000 women registered to vote, which represents between 16 and 20 percent of the eligible female voting population. Almost everyone interviewed, both women and men, characterized this percentage as significant and positive considering these were the first multiparty elections for the newly unified country. The registration of women, therefore, was perceived as a glass 20 percent full rather than 80 percent empty. Nonetheless, there is evidence that the rate of participation could have been significantly higher if the SEC and political leaders had made a concerted effort to encourage women's participation in the electoral process.

Levels of female registration varied among governorates throughout the country. For example, in the southern cities of Aden and Taiz, women accounted for 35 percent and 20 percent of registered voters respectively. However, in the northern city of Hajja, the number of females who registered represented only 9 percent. In Sadah this figure was 3 percent. A more conservative, tribal culture in Hajja and Sadah may partially explain the variance, but figures in nearby constituencies within the same governorates were equally discordant. Within some districts in the governorate of Taiz, for instance, female registration reached 30 percent, whereas only 5 percent of eligible female voters registered in other districts.

The NDI delegation concluded that efforts by certain political parties and candidates to recruit female voters represented the strongest determinant in creating the disparate registration levels within a governorate. Yemeni women frequently mentioned al-Islah as the most active and effective party in this respect. Some such initiatives were clearly permitted under the law, while others appeared to violate the election code. Frequently, the "get-out-the-vote" efforts depended on the passivity, compliance or ignorance of the women involved. The NDI team heard from registration officials, two female independent candidates and an eligible voter that the three major political parties (most frequently al-Islah) had purchased thousands of citizen identification cards from Civil Ministry employees who had personal affiliations with the various parties.

Eventually, these cards were used to illegally register both men and women who were either from another district or under the legal voting age.

Two different groups of women who had worked as officials at registration sites told stories about women who were bused to sites to register. Though female registration officials recognized that these women either were not from the district or were younger than the legal voting age, men accompanying the women, often a village leader or a political party representative, insisted they be registered. The registration officials complied.

One group of female registration officials who had worked in a district outside of Sana'a strongly believed that the majority of women who registered were manipulated by either the political parties or candidates. They related accounts of women asking where they could pick up food rations that had been promised to them in exchange for registering. Other women arrived at the registration center prepared to vote for a certain candidate, whose name their husband or father had given them. A third group of women, government workers, were allegedly told by superiors in the work place that their salaries would be withheld until they produced proof of registration.

All of these accounts suggest that the low level of comprehension of the election process by women may have made the exercise less than meaningful for them even when they did participate. While the same is true of many men, it does seem that women were more vulnerable to manipulation and misunderstanding due to their disadvantaged social status.

Mobilizing citizens to vote is a standard campaign endeavor. Nonetheless, evidence suggests that many Yemeni women voted solely at the prompting of other people or parties and not as a free expression of interest or preference. Al-Islah successfully recruited female members to vote but later asked its women members to withdraw their candidacies as well as their support for other female candidates. One al-Islah leader, with whom the NDI team met, proudly spoke of the party's success in involving large numbers of women in the political process. Upon hearing that claim, a female civic leader claimed that al-Islah "merely used the women as tools."

The women who worked on registration committees often faced significant obstacles, beginning with the manner in which they were trained. Male registration officials were trained directly by government officials. These local men were in turn asked to teach the women. Women interviewed believed that their training, once removed from the professional source, was of lower quality than that provided to men. Two women also told the NDI delegation that they were threatened with the loss of their jobs if they worked on the committees. Several female registration officials stated that they had tolerated verbal harassment from soldiers stationed at registration sites. Incidents of physical violence against women at two sites in the Sana'a area were also reported.

After assessing the barriers to women's registration, the NDI delegation divided them into two categories, institutional and cultural. Institutional impediments arise from the structure of the election system itself. Cultural obstacles relate variously to misogynous interpretations of religious tradition, tribal customs, and habits of social and economic organization.

## Institutional Obstacles to Women's Participation as Voters

It is not clear whether the separate facilities legally prescribed for women's participation in the elections would necessarily encourage or discourage female participation. The delegation heard conflicting views, although most people agreed that there is a comfort level associated with gender segregation that probably would have eased women into the process. However, it was equally clear that separate was not equal. In fact, the provision of opportunity to women was distinctly inferior to the opportunity afforded to men.

Many registration centers for women opened after more than two weeks into the four-week registration period, and some sites were not established until three days before the period ended. The tardy opening of women's registration sites undoubtedly led to lower female participation than would have otherwise been the case.

When asked about this belatedness, two members of the SEC acknowledged the problem. By way of explanation they told the delegation that they "were not able to recruit an adequate number of women" to staff the registration sites. However, the Yemen Women's Union and some of the political parties claimed they had submitted to the SEC lists of "hundreds of women" who were willing to work on the registration process. Staffing a registration site was a popular job, as it included a daily salary regarded quite ample by

Yemeni standards. Apparently, very few of these women had been contacted by the SEC officials. One female member of the YSP asserted that the "SEC has played a great role in inhibiting women's participation in the process." This statement reflects the attitude of a large number of women interviewed toward the SEC's role in administering the elections.

One member of the SEC affirmed that women's registration was not a priority for the majority of SEC members and suspected that ulterior motives caused the procedural delay. Three female candidates interviewed by the delegation alleged that, by the time the SEC was politically forced to address the problem (in part because the SEC and the government were embarrassed by international scrutiny), the funds originally allocated for this purpose had already been spent.

The majority of urban women interviewed characterized as ineffective the SEC's attempt to use the media to encourage women's participation. Moreover, women from rural areas told the NDI delegation that they were completely uninformed about the registration process; they did not know where, how or why to register. Even those who reported having seen the television appeals targeted to women considered them too infrequent and unconvincing. One independent candidate wrote a newspaper article questioning the SEC's sincerity. She urged SEC members and political party leaders to put their own wives and daughters on television as examples of women's participation. Her entreaty went unheeded.

A modest grassroots effort to encourage women to vote was initiated by the Yemen Women's Union. The leadership instructed branch leaders to talk to women about registration, but the officials told the NDI delegation that "funding was limited, and we could not do what was needed for women."

The great distances required of citizens to travel to reach registration sites posed an additional obstacle to women's registration. Each constituency, averaging 21,000 eligible voters, comprised four to six registration centers, usually located in schools or other public buildings. The complaint about inferior proximity and accessibility was repeated by men as well as women. However, given the cultural restraints imposed upon women's mobility outside the home, the faraway sites undoubtedly affected women's registration more than men's.

The requirement that two photographs be taken of each registrant represented another important procedural barrier to women's registration. The election law requires that one photo be provided for the identification card. Instant cameras were part of the registration equipment, and photos were taken on-site. However, due to the short period of time remaining before the April 27 elections, the SEC required registrars to produce two photos. One was to be used as a temporary registration card, which was to remain with the voter to be used on election day. The other photo was to be kept with the SEC in order to be used when issuing permanent registration cards for future elections.

There exists in Yemen a rigid social stigma against photographing women, most of whom customarily wear full veils, (*lithma*), in public. Rumors spread about possible "abuses" that could occur with the extra SEC photo. One woman told the delegation, "Most husbands will not even allow the names of their wives to be uttered in conversation. How can we expect them to accept that their wife's picture will be taken and kept in an unknown place?"

An SEC official who spoke with the NDI team claimed that the extra picture issue was an irrelevant matter. She explained that men do not object to the photographs of their wives required for driver's licenses or passports. She suggested that the same parties that mobilized women to register simultaneously spread rumors about the photos so that other parties would bar their female relatives and associates from registering to vote.

### Cultural Obstacles to Women's Participation as Voters

The cultural obstacles to the registration of women, as well as to any kind of political participation by women, were extensive. One female independent candidate told the NDI team that "traditions are against women. I am treated like a citizen from the second degree, although this is not written anywhere." This perception of inferiority, recognized by both men and women, affects not only the role of women in society but also relations between men and women. Since cultural traditions forbid virtually any male-female interaction in the public realm, women are excluded and ultimately isolated from many aspects of civic and political life. "People are still not convinced that women should have lives outside of their home," professed one female member of the PGC.

Public segregation of men and women forces women to seek authority and respect in the private domain; the role of women in society is confined to domestic activities. Social networks are important channels through which women define and implement their role. These networks, such as neighborhood groups and *qat* sessions, are frequently based on friendship and familial relations. It is within this context that women are able to express their authority and articulate their opinions. One independent female candidate dismissed her husband as "no good" when describing the management of her household. However, given the cultural restrictions placed on male-female relations in public, "men can not even say women are qualified, even when the men think the women are. People would say 'there is a love affair.' People are afraid of rumors."

Not surprisingly, the NDI team noted a feeling of indifference toward the electoral process among many of the women interviewed. Many did not feel included in the process, nor did they believe that they would be affected by it. As one woman put it, "Why should women be any more involved in the elections than they are in making decisions in their own homes — or anywhere else in this country?"

A government official, who surveyed women in villages where she works, recounted the most common reason given by women for not registering: "My husband is away. I cannot register without his permission. He would divorce me." Indeed, the NDI team was told of three cases in Taiz where husbands divorced their wives because the women had registered without spousal permission. Many women who registered of their own accord spoke about the physical and mental repercussions of taking such a step. The chairman of an SEC supervisory committee in Ibb summed up the situation when he noted, "There is a perception that women are involved in domestic work and do not have time to think about political activities. The husband's responsibility is to participate in the political process for both of them."

### Women in Leadership

Discussions regarding women currently in leadership positions provoked references to several female leaders of the Arab world including Yemen. Yemen's first female ruler was Queen Belgiza of

Sheba who ruled approximately 2,000 years ago. Her belief in the democratic principle of popular participation led to the establishment of an informal consultative structure of government; citizens were consulted before policy decisions were made. Another well-known female leader was A'isha, the wife of the Prophet Mohammed. After the death of the Prophet, A'isha led an armed revolt in AD 632 against the caliph who ruled at that time. Her leadership skills eventually contributed to the downfall of the fourth caliph during what is called the "Battle of the Camel," referring to the camel ridden by A'isha. These women, historically significant in Yemen, demonstrate that women not only have rights but also serve as reminders of strong female leadership.

Though *sharia* (Islamic law) does not explicitly prohibit women from holding leadership positions in Yemeni society, it is undeniable that impediments exist. The 1993 elections reduced the number of women in parliament from 10 to two, a common phenomenon internationally when countries move from one-party systems to multiparty elections. There are no female ministers or deputy ministers; women have only been appointed to the level of assistant deputy minister. There are several female judges in southern Yemen but none in northern Yemen, and there is apparently only one practicing female lawyer in northern Yemen.

Many Yemenis attribute the under-representation of women in positions of leadership to the conservative, tribal social structure. Most women, particularly in northern Yemen are not encouraged to complete their education, a status that disqualifies them from many jobs. Promoting education for women was a government priority in the former People's Democratic Republic of Yemen in the South, although that commitment is not yet apparent in the unified government. Even for women who do join political, professional or civic organizations, domestic responsibilities often preclude qualified women from seeking leadership positions. Several women spoke of the reluctance on the part of many men to associate professionally with women in the work place due to a social stigma that discourages friendships between unrelated men and women.

Once women attain certain positions of leadership, cultural tradition often limits their effectiveness. For instance, SEC meetings conducted during Ramadan did not include the only female member of the Committee. These meetings were held either after dark when women generally do not leave their homes or during *qat* sessions from which, as previously stated, women are effectively excluded.

Male political party leaders often argue that women "choose" not to seek positions of leadership in politics, despite male support and encouragement. A PGC leader and member of the Presidential Council reiterated this view to the NDI delegation. Even though Yemen's constitution grants equal access to all professions, the political parties do not appreciate that they should, nor do they understand how they can, increase women's participation. The PGC, for instance, nominated only the two women, whom they "thought would have a chance to win." However, the PGC also requested that several high-ranking female members of the party withdraw their candidacies in other districts on the grounds that "the competition would be too much trouble for them." A leader of the al-Islah party was ambivalent about the necessity of including women in leadership positions. He explained, "Women don't have to be in the party leadership to be taken care of." Even high officials of the avowedly egalitarian Yemeni Socialist Party (YSP) appeared to share the view that women should not be exposed to the rough and tumble of electoral politics.

When asked whether the YSP would present women as candidates, one senior official responded in the affirmative (at which point his wife, who was present, smiled in amusement and apparent disbelief). He then offered a caveat. The YSP would only nominate women in those districts where they stood a good chance to win — so as not to subject women to "the humiliation of failure." In response to further questioning, the official then said that he did not think women stood a good chance in urban areas, nor in rural areas — and he could not identify one place where he believed that a woman could realistically expect to win a competitive election.

PGC leaders who spoke with the NDI delegation lauded their own party's support for several independent female candidates, one of whom the delegation subsequently interviewed. She explained, however, that the PGC's "support" was a simple agreement whereby the party would allow her to be a candidate and not directly attack her. Meanwhile, the PGC nominated a male candidate in the same district, and provided him with both political and financial support. This male candidate eventually won more than 50 percent of the vote, whereas the independent female candidate "supported" by the PGC won less than 2 percent.

Deciding whether or not to run for parliament was a difficult choice for Yemen's few prominent women, as the prospects of winning a seat were remote. They were openly discouraged by party leaders from running on the party lists, which obliged them to run as independents relying on personal resources. One independent female candidate, when acknowledging the support of her husband, told the NDI team, "If I win a seat in parliament, at least he will know where I am everyday." Women who have some experience in public affairs expressed frustration. They professed: "If I'm not going to win, why should I contest?" and "The effect is minimal compared to the effort. I'm tired." At the same time, men of promise and pro-minence were actively recruited by the principal parties to align with them rather than contest the elections as independents.

Several female candidates, however, told the NDI team that they were involved principally to demonstrate that women were interested and able. If women declined the challenge at this juncture, they insisted, male leaders would label them passive. One said, "Women should have stood as candidates as a principle — even if they thought they would lose." Two others proclaimed, "If we are still living, next time we will run for local council."

Some male leaders interviewed by the delegation insist that there are currently no women who are experienced and well-educated enough for high-level positions. However, several women with whom the delegation met, claimed that they frequently possessed higher formal qualifications and more years of experience than their male superiors at the government departments or ministries where they work.

Several women interviewed spoke of tokenism as a tactic used by the current political leaders to appease local and international groups concerned about the meager representation of women in leadership positions. Indeed, when the NDI delegation broached the subject of barriers to women's political leadership, male leaders tended to recite the names of the same four or five women as proof that there are no obstacles other than "Yemeni cultural backwardness" and that the majority of women "are not used to" or "not qualified for" such work. But several women countered that argument by explaining that "80 percent of the problem [impediments to women in leadership] is tradition. Men don't want their women to work, to leave the house." Those women who do hold leadership positions are perceived to be part of the "democratic decoration." One female civic leader complained, "I don't want to be part of the decor. I want my real rights." Another civic leader, who had watched parliament in session on television for six weeks and never heard a woman speak, lamented, "I can do more for women in the field than those women sitting in parliament."

The NDI delegation explored with the Yemen Women's Union the possibility of the Union serving as a potential voice for the particular interests of women and as a source of female political leaders. Before unification, the Yemen Women's Union in the North comprised a loose configuration of politically and economically disparate groups. The structure of the Yemen Women's Union in the South, however, was more cohesive. It occupied ministry status, and its executive board enjoyed full-time, paid positions. The leadership was both appointed and supervised by the governing party. Although the board designed projects to meet the needs of women and solicited funding from international development organizations, it was greatly influenced by the governing Yemeni Socialist Party.

At times this arrangement was viewed in a positive light. For example, the Union worked in conjunction with the YSP to implement projects for women such as conducting literacy campaigns and establishing technical training and skills/crafts centers. On other occasions, the Union was constrained and regulated by the YSP and was unable to act independently. The YSP was successful, however, in encouraging women to participate and to become actively involved in the Union's activities, which gave credence to its work. It is important to note that despite the active involvement of many citizens, the leadership of the Yemen Women's Union was never democratically elected.

Since unification, the potential power and influence of the Yemen Women's Union has been steadily reduced by the political parties. A long-time member of the Union sadly reported, "We lost many things after unification." Women who formerly served in the leadership of the Women's Union in the South were dispersed among various ministries. The Union was placed under the control of the Ministry of Planning and the Ministry of Social Affairs, through which the executive board must channel all activities and requests for international assistance. The Ministry of Planning administered new elections for the unified Union. Several members claimed that the results of these elections were predetermined and were conducted in the presence of a selected audience. In order to address the threats to the integrity of the organization, one woman argued, "The leadership of the Yemen Women's Union has to be changed and selected by the women in the Union at the grassroots level."

### Islamic Law, Democracy and Women

Islamic law (*sharia*) is explicitly the foundation for Yemen's judicial system. Yemen's leaders interpret the *sharia* to formulate laws and define the legal rights of the citizen. The fact that Yemen's leadership is universally male means that women generally do not have a voice in influencing the way the *sharia* is interpreted and hence do not participate in shaping their own legal rights. In fact, the increasingly restrictive interpretation of the *sharia* by the government may be the dominant factor limiting women from full participation in Yemeni civic and political life.

Specific to Islamic law, the NDI delegation was interested in learning women's opinions on two questions: Can there be democracy in an Islamic state? In an Islamic state, could or should the *sharia* be interpreted in a more egalitarian manner than is currently realized in Yemen?

One woman interviewed held that Islamic law itself subjugates women and, for this reason, there could be no genuine democracy in Muslim Yemen. Yet, only one woman of the dozens interviewed directly criticized the negative effects of Islamic law on women. Neither men nor women were prepared to discuss the sociological implications of Islam with respect to the role of women in society and politics. When a member of the delegation asked a Yemeni woman for her opinion on polygamy she turned to her friend and asked, "Why is she pressing on with polygamy, what has it got to do with political participation?"

The vast majority of those interviewed maintained that democracy is possible in an Islamic state. However, they agreed that the type of democracy would depend on the interpretation of the *sharia* used to formulate law. An independent female candidate for parliament offered, "The *sharia* originally meant justice for all, but now it needs reinterpretation."

Many women believe that Islam is, and can be, flexible with respect to specific policy issues. They acknowledge that the *sharia* has been interpreted differently throughout the world. They believe that, if there were to emerge a popular consensus regarding equal rights for women, the *sharia* can and should accommodate popular opinion.

It is important to note that official interpretations of the *sharia* have varied throughout Yemeni history. Many male and female Yemenis interviewed mentioned that a tendency toward religious conservativism in northern Yemen has been increasingly apparent since the 1979 revolution in Iran. The more frequent use of the veil by women represents the most obvious manifestation of this direction. Government and religious leaders strongly encouraged the use of the veil through the educational system and television. Simultaneously in the South, the opposite was being promoted as the communist government encouraged women to remove the veil. Since unification, northern influences have dominated the cultural climate, and more and more young women wear veils.

During NDI's various meetings in Aden and elsewhere in southern Yemen, it was not uncommon for mother and daughter to arrive together, the mother in Western clothing with no veil and the daughter fully covered. Women who were once influential government officials from the South arrived to work in the unified government in the new capital of Sana'a only to find that they were expected to conform to new, conservative standards of dress and demeanor. One female government official from South Yemen recounted the extensive harassment she encountered in the work place when she began a job in northern Yemen in 1990; until she relented, stopped wearing makeup and put on the veil.

Before unification, the People's Democratic Republic of Yemen (PDRY) established a Family Law that delineated conditions for marriage contracts. This law prohibited pre-arranged marriages by the parents of the bride-to-be. The bride was required to be at least 16 years old at the time of marriage, and the groom was to be at least 18 and not more than 20 years older than the bride. This law also obliged the registration of marriages, limited the price charged for the bride and restricted polygamy. The husband's right to divorce his wife by simple repudiation was abolished, and grounds for divorce were equalized for husbands and wives. Finally, divorced mothers gained the right to retain custody of their children until the son was at least 10 years old and the daughter at least 15 years old, at which time the courts could ascertain the child's wishes in the matter.

In May 1992, the unified Presidential Council under President Saleh bypassed the legislature and issued a Personal Status Law, Republican Decree No. 20. This law revoked a woman's right to sue for divorce unless she could prove that her husband was abusive (though many women related accounts of a woman waiting years for the court to make a decision only to have her request be denied); allowed husbands to divorce their wives without justifying it to the court (and in some cases of divorce, the family home and children are automatically awarded to the husband); re-introduced the acceptance of polygamy; and eliminated the PDRY ceiling on the price of the bride. Various parliamentarians and jurists objected to this decree, as well as to the manner of its enactment, which prompted a curious instance of civil disobedience by judges. A group of jurists from Aden in Southern Yemen refused to implement the law and questioned the constitutionality of the decree.

Interpretations of the *sharia* adopted in Iran, Turkey, Tunisia, Saudi Arabia, Bangladesh and other Muslim countries were discussed during interviews with the NDI delegation. They were all viewed by Yemeni women differently — too strict, too lenient, or inappropriate for Yemen's situation. Several Yemeni women referred vaguely to "enlightened interpretations" of the *sharia* that encourage women to participate in political life. But efforts to ascertain what these enlightened interpretations could mean to specific issues in Yemen led to vague discussions.

While examining the topic of the *sharia* as it affects women's rights, one male leader of al-Islah repeated several times that "there would be no debate if only everyone understood the true meaning of the *sharia*." Yet he was unable to explain who should interpret the *sharia* and whether one interpretation should prevail over another. He was also unclear about how the "true meaning" of the *sharia* would affect women. However, his answers to a series of questions implied that the status of women would most likely worsen. For instance, when pressed about the issue of divorce rights, the political leader acknowledged that he does not approve of the right to an equal divorce process for men and women. His reasoning was based on his belief that "women are too emotional" and might request a divorce "without thinking it through properly."

Questions specific to divorce rights, inheritance law, polygamy, marital age and other areas were answered differently by everyone, depending on personal beliefs. For example, regarding the issue of polygamy, many men and one woman viewed it simply as an integral part of Islam. But the vast majority of women who spoke with the delegation believed that it should be prohibited in practice. They reasoned that the Koran states that a man is allowed to have more than one wife, *provided he treats them equally*. According to these women, logic and experience dictates that it is impossible to treat more than one wife equally, and therefore polygamy should not be practiced.

When pressed to make a comparison between the former PDRY's Family Law and the more recent Personal Status Law, all of the women interviewed by the delegation, with the one exception, preferred the former law because of its more egalitarian treatment of women. Those women originally from the South were particularly adamant in their responses and were incredulous that unification "has taken us backward." One woman, however, who was part of the committee that wrote the compromise that was implemented in Decree No. 20, believed it was an appropriate compromise and represented at least a positive first step for women in the North.

Several women who spoke to the NDI delegation expressed the view that Islam is used by certain political parties and religious leaders to justify tribal conservativism and the oppression of women. An election official declared, "Islam becomes an excuse to keep women down and keep them passive." However, she argued, it is the sacred nature of Islamic law that prevents the majority of women and men from reaching that same conclusion; as Islam is sacred, it cannot be linked to oppression. This special standing prevents individuals from questioning or challenging certain aspects of the law that oppress women.

If women were to unite and demand a reinterpretation of the *sharia* in order to reach social equity, they would certainly clash with very powerful, conservative tribal factions of society. An even more serious question is whether any legal consensus on reinterpretation of the *sharia*, or a reworking of the Personal Status Law, could ever be enforced given the dubious independence of the judicial system. As one female government official told the delegation, the judiciary currently "applies the law as it suits men."

The delegation concluded that there is a strong relationship between the manner in which Islamic law is interpreted in Yemen and the extent of women's participation in civic and political life. Religious leaders, and politicians influenced by them, have used conservative interpretations of Islam to inhibit women from assuming responsibilities and positions of leadership outside the domestic realm. NDI team member Arat stated, "I believe the fundamental problem is not Islam but patriarchal authoritarianism that Islam helps legitimize..." The male leadership's interpretation of Islamic law places restrictions on women's lives. The lack of visible, active women in political and social life contributes to predominant social doubt regarding the appropriateness and qualifications of women to be leaders. This apprehension creates an ominous force to prohibit women from having a voice in the country's newfound multiparty political system.

## C. Conclusions

1) There was a widely held belief among women interviewed that the principal political parties predetermined the results of the elections through political deals. Nevertheless, the introduction of a multiparty system and the 1993 elections, with all of its imperfections, inspired a notable public optimism for the possibility of true democracy in Yemen.

2) Illiteracy, which disproportionately affects women, was a significant obstacle to becoming an informed voter.

3) Women's participation in the Yemeni election process was significant relative to nearby countries, although it remained far from realizing its full potential. Registering 20 percent of eligible female voters appears to be an impressive first experience for Yemen. However, it is equally clear that the SEC substantially failed to fulfill its legal mandate to incorporate women as full participants in the election process. Had the SEC conducted an educational program targeted toward women and their specific concerns regarding the registration process, the registration figure would have undoubtedly risen.

4) Women are under represented in the leadership of the political and social institutions of Yemen. In addition, many of the few women who do occupy positions of leadership have not been afforded full participation rights in the developing electoral process.

5) There is a widely held belief by male political leaders that women specifically choose not to be involved in the political process, particularly at higher levels, such as running for public office. The NDI delegation, however, met several apparently qualified women who have in fact unsuccessfully sought such positions. In instances where women have opted not to pursue leadership roles, the choice is often a function of their deep alienation from the system.

6) The practice of certain fundamental democratic rights guaranteed in the Universal Declaration of Human Rights (freedom of expression and association) is especially difficult for women in Yemen due to currently prevailing interpretation(s) of Islamic law.

7) There exists no current vehicle, including any genuinely non-governmental organization, through which women can participate in political and civic life.

## D. Recommendations

1) In the future, the parliament and the Supreme Election Committee can and should encourage female registration through all available means and must make registration accessible to all women.

2) All social institutions, including the government, political parties and non-governmental organizations, should strive to eliminate barriers to women's participation in the election process. Before future elections, women should be targeted in campaigns to promote registration. Subsequently, there should be a public effort undertaken to educate registered women about the issues, candidates and election-day procedures.

3) All political education campaigns should consider the special needs of illiterate voters and emphasize the concept of a secret ballot.

4) Considering the much higher rates of illiteracy for women and girls, they should be targeted for adequate education by the government of Yemen and by the international donor community. The delegation strongly believes that the education of girls and boys should remain integrated in the interest of affording both groups the same quality education and opportunity for choice regarding all aspects of personal growth. Segregation in the schools, as has been proposed by some Yemenis, would likely lead to the further marginalization of women in society. Separate educational facilities would not be equal.

5) The education of women was considered vital by all interviewed, but education and professional experience alone are insufficient to afford women access to leadership positions in Yemen. Rather, there must emerge an institutional consensus that women belong in these positions.

6) Once women have reached positions of leadership, efforts must be made on the part of male leaders to ensure female presence at all levels, and in all forums, of decision-making.

7) International organizations should support those women currently in leadership positions as well as indigenous groups striving to support women at the local, regional and national levels. A special emphasis should be placed on training women to organize independent citizen groups that could influence the political process. For example, the delegation recommends offering a training program that acquaints women with political organizations and interest groups from other countries.

8) The delegation recommends conducting a more systematic and detailed survey to determine the attitudes of Yemeni women and men about issues of equity and citizenship. Such an initiative would help form the basis for properly focused civic education programs about democratic citizenship.

9) International groups should bring Islamic intellectuals to Yemen who could share and popularize information about how to reconcile democracy with Islamic tradition, not only in theory but in practice.

10) International groups, Yemeni citizens and the SEC should work together to establish a target figure for increased levels of female registration for the next elections. To achieve their objective,

the SEC should sponsor and implement a long-term voter education and registration campaign in preparation for the next local or national elections.

11) At the request of several Yemeni leaders, this report should be widely disseminated, in both English and Arabic.

## Chapter 5

# Conclusion

---

After many years in which the two Yemeni states were buffeted and used by more powerful governments — both in the Arab world and at the superpower level — Yemenis now find themselves able to chart their nation's future free from decisive outside intervention. The future of democracy in Yemen will be determined by Yemenis.

Many Yemenis remain concerned that the monarchs of the Gulf want their democratic experiment to fail. Others are uneasy that pan-Arab movements, including both the Syrian and Iraqi Ba'athist parties and Islamists based variously in Sudan, Egypt and Iran, desire to control Yemeni politics. International relations for this rather isolated country have been complicated by the demise of the Soviet Union, which was for two decades the patron and financier of South Yemen, and the consequent diminishing of Western interest in the North. The Gulf War presented the united Yemen with difficult and costly choices — and led to its estrangement from Saudi Arabia and Kuwait.

The elections of April 1993 represent a significant step in the direction of democratic and accountable politics, despite the various shortcomings that were manifest in the process. Unfortunately, internal political developments since then have not led to further consolidation of the nascent pluralist system. A confrontation between the leaders of the significant parties — the People's General Congress and the Yemeni Socialist Party — escalated to crisis proportion in the last few months of the year. The very unity of the nation, which was to have been sealed by the legislative elections, has been jeopardized. The unification of the two prior states' armies and other institutions has been stalled or reversed. In December, Vice President Ali Salim al-Bidh proposed that both he and President Ali Abdullah Saleh resign in order to defuse the crisis. While this development has not happened, Yemen's Foreign Minister Mohammed Basindwah told the press in early December that "there is an unannounced split. The only thing left is to declare the split."

So Yemen's democratic achievements to date remain precarious accomplishments. Those who support the process of democratization and internal Yemeni reconciliation should renew their willingness to respond to requests from the people of Yemen.

# APPENDICES

*Appendix I*

# Yemen Election Results
## April 27, 1993

| Party | Number of Votes | Percentage of Total Votes | Number of Seats Won |
|---|---|---|---|
| PGC | 624,151 | 29 | 122 |
| YSP | 402,725 | 18 | 54 |
| ISLAH | 362,201 | 17 | 62 |
| BAATH | 74,404 | 3 | 6 |
| NASIRIST | 12,527 | 1 | 4 |
| AL-HAQQ | 16,599 | 1 | 2 |
| Other Parties | 71,151 | 3 | 0 |
| Independent Winners | 172,644 | 8 | 50 |
| Other Independents | 443,540 | 20 | 0 |
| Total | 2,179,942 | 100 | 300 * |

* 301 seats in the body; election was suspended at mid-day in Hodeida district 192.

*Source: Supreme Election Committee*

*Appendix II*

# Letters of Invitation to NDI to Work in Yemen from Foreign Minister Al-Eryani

December 23, 1992

Mr. Thomas O. Melia                    VIA FACSIMILE
Program Director
National Democratic Institute
 for International Affairs
1717 Massachusetts Avenue, N.W.
Suite 605
Washington, D.C. 20036

Dear Mr. Melia:

I understand that the National Democratic Institute for International Affairs (NDI) is considering sending a pre-election delegation to Yemen in January. The government of Yemen is greatly encouraged by NDI's interest in the elections in Yemen and NDI's willingness to lend its expertise to our electoral process.

As we discussed in Washington, the Government of Yemen would like to receive advice regarding the administration of voting for military personnel and regarding difficulties associated with female participation in the electoral process, both as candidates and in balloting. It would also be useful if the delegation would address the issue of the role of coalitions in a parliamentary system, possibly as part of a seminar on political parties. Of course, I understand that you will want to meet with election officials, party officials, candidates, human rights groups, and others during your visit. The Government of Yemen will make every effort to assist in facilitating these meetings, if that would be helpful. Please feel free to contact me through John Babb at Baker & Botts or the U.S. Embassy in Sana'a on or after January 16.

I look forward to seeing you in Sana'a in January and again express the government of Yemen's appreciation for NDI's interest and efforts in connection with the upcoming April elections.

Very truly yours,

Dr. Abdul Karim Al-Eryani
Deputy Prime Minister
Minister of Foreign Affairs

[received in Washington January 20, 1993]

Mr. Thomas O. Melia
Program Director
National Democratic Institute
 for International Affairs
1717 Massachusetts Avenue, N.W.
Suite 605
Washington, D.C. 20036

Dear Mr. Melia:

I understand that the National Democratic Institute for International Affairs (NDI) is considering sending additional pre-election delegations to Yemen in February, March and April. The government of Yemen is greatly encouraged by NDI's interest in the elections in Yemen and NDI's willingness to lend its expertise to our electoral process.

As we discussed in Washington and during your recent visit to Sana'a, the Government of Yemen welcomes these delegations organized by NDI. I understand that you will want to meet with election officials, party officials, candidates, human rights groups, and others during your visit. The Government of Yemen will make every effort to assist in facilitating these meetings, if that would be helpful.

Please consider this letter an invitation to you and your colleagues at NDI, and also to those experts and delegates that you may invite to join your team from the U.S. and other countries. By this letter, I would request the embassies of Yemen abroad to cooperate in the provision of visas to NDI's delegations.

I look forward to seeing you back in Sana'a and again express the Government of Yemen's appreciation for NDI's interest and efforts in connection with the upcoming April elections.

Very truly yours,

Dr. Abdul Karim Al-Eryani
Deputy Prime Minister
Minister of Foreign Affairs

*Appendix III*

# Delegation Schedule
## First Pre-Election Mission
## January 27 to February 2, 1993

## Thursday, January 27, 1993

| | |
|---|---|
| 8 am | Arthur Hughes, U.S. Ambassador to Yemen<br>George Flores, Director of U.S. AID<br>Bruce Strathearn, Deputy Chief of Mission<br>John Lister, Political Officer |
| 10 am | People's General Congress Party (PGC)<br>Dr. Yahya Al-Mutawakkil, Permanent Committee of PGC<br>Dr. Abdul Salim Al-Ansi, Organizer,<br>    Public Committee of PGC |
| 11 am | Mr. Ali Salem Al-Bidh, Vice President and<br>    Secretary General, Yemeni Socialist Party |
| 3 pm | Qat Session<br>Members of the National Conference<br>Dr. Abdulmalek Al-Mutawakkil, Vice Chairman<br>    of Association for the Defense of Human Rights<br>    and Freedom<br>Mr. Mohamed A. Fusial, Member of Parliament<br>    (PGC)<br>Dr. Ahmed Al-Kaizimi, Sana'a University,<br>    Chairman of Association for the Defense of<br>    Human Rights and Freedom<br>Dr. Abdul Hamid Al-Sharif, Sana'a University<br>Dr. Salem Bkair, Central Committee YSP<br>Dr. Abdullah Al-Hrabei, Permanent Committee<br>    PGC<br>Dr. Abdul Rahman Al-Jafri, President of Sons of<br>    Yemen League<br>Dr. Ahmed Al-Kibsi, PGC, Chairman Yemeni<br>    Political Science Association<br>Dr. Abdul Kodus Al-Mudwiah, United Nasserist |

Party
Dr. Abdul Wahab Al-Ansi, Secretary General of
Al Islah Party
Mr. Malek Al-Iryani, Secretary YSP (Sana'a)
Mr. Salem Amar Hussein, Deputy Minister of
Information, Aden Branch
Dr. Ayhub A. Ahmed, Sana'a University
Mr. Shar M. Salem, Ministry of Legal Affairs
Mr. Ahmed Al-Sharmi, President of Al-Haqq

## Friday, January 28, 1993

| | |
|---|---|
| 11 am | Visit registration site in Taiz |
| 1:30 pm | Arrive Aden |
| | Luncheon with the Yemeni Socialist Party (YSP) |
| | Mr. Saleh Shaif, Secretary, Aden Branch |
| | Mr. Othman Kamaran, Deputy Governor |
| 3:30 pm | Mr. Hisham Bashraheel, Publisher, *Al-Ayyam* |
| | Mr. Tammam Bashraheel, Editor, *Al-Ayyam* |
| 5 pm | Qat Session with Members of the Association for the Defense of Human Rights and Freedom (ADHRF) |
| | Dr. Ahmed Mohammed Al-Kaizimi, Chairman |
| | Mr. Salem Omer Hussein, Vice Chairman, Aden Branch |
| | Dr. Ahmed Hussein Bilal, Secretary of Foreign Relations |
| | Mr. Anwar Khaled, Chairman, Aden |
| | Mr. Nassir Ali-Nasser, Vice Chairman, Aden Branch |
| | Abdul Ellah Al-Marwani, Lawyer |
| | Mokbil Haidara, Lawyer |

## Saturday, January 30, 1993

| | |
|---|---|
| 11:30 am | Shaikh Abdullah Bin Hussein Al-Ahmer, Leader, Al Islah Party |
| | Mr. Abdullah Al-Akwa, Member of Parliament |
| 1 pm | Luncheon with the National Conference |
| 4 pm | Mr. Mohammed A. Abuluhum, M.P., Leader of the Republican Party |

## Sunday, January 31, 1993

| | |
|---|---|
| 8:30 am | Dr. Mohammed Abdulmalek Al-Mutawakkil<br>Mr. Mustapha Noman, Chairman of Yemeni National Committee for Free Elections (NCFE) |
| 11 am | Supreme Election Committee<br>Mr. Abdul Kareem Al-Arashi, Chairman, Member of the Presidential Council |
| 2:30 pm | Luncheon with Sons of Yemen League Party<br>Dr. Abdul Rahman Ali Al-Jafri, President<br><br>Melissa Estok: Lunch with Mrs. Al-Jafri, Anisa Othman, Mrs. Al-Nur |
| 7 pm | Dinner with the Electoral Reform Society (ERS) and the International Foundation for Electoral Systems (IFES) |

## Monday, February 1, 1993

| | |
|---|---|
| 8:30 am | Yemeni-American Friendship Association<br>Dr. Raufa Hassan Al-Sharki, Deputy Chairperson<br>Mr. Jamal Al-Muttareb, Member |
| 10:15 am | Dr. Abdul Karim Al-Eryani, Minister of Foreign Affairs |
| 12 noon | University of Sana'a<br>Dr. Monsir Al-Zandani, Chairman, Political Science Department<br>Dr. Ahmed Al-Kibsi, Chairman, Yemeni Political Science Association<br>Dr. Abdul Sharif, Political Science Department, Deputy Dean<br>Dr. Mohammed Abdulmalek Al-Mutawakkil, M.P., National Conference<br>Mr. Mustapha Noman, Chairman, NCFE<br>Mr. Ahmed Mohammed Al-Uthman, NCFE |
| 1:30 pm | Lunch with Shaekh Abdullah Bin Hussein Al-Ahmer, Leader of Al Islah Party |
| 5 pm | Thomas Melia: U.S. Embassy<br>Ambassador Arthur Hughes |

George Flores, U.S. AID
Larry Dominessey, U.S. AID
Keith Kline, IFES
Ron Wolfe, IFES

Melissa Estok: Ministry of Information
Amat Al-Alim Al-Soswa, Assistant Deputy
Minister

## Tuesday, February 2, 1993

| | |
|---|---|
| 11 am | Visit to Parliament |
| 12 noon | Mr. Ayat Noman, <br> Advisor to Mr. Abdul Aziz Abdul-Gani, <br> Member of the Presidential Council |
| 1 pm | Mr. Ahmed Al-Eryani, Office of the President, <br> Central Organization for Auditing |
| 2:15 pm | Supreme Electoral Commission <br> Ms. Raqia Homaydan, Independent |
| 6:30 pm | Mr. Omar Al-Jawi, YSP <br> Mr. Salem Saleh Mohammed, YSP |
| 7:30 pm | Supreme Election Committee <br> Mr. Saiq Amin Abdullah Rais, Head of the <br> Technical Committee, Minister of Agriculture <br> and Water <br> Mr. Abdul Malek Al-Mikhlafy, Head of <br> Information Committee |

*Appendix IV*

# Letter from NDI Survey Mission Leader John Bruton to SEC

January 31, 1993

Al-Qadi Abdul Karim Al-Arashi
Member, Presidential Council
Chairman, Supreme Election Committee
Sana'a, Republic of Yemen

Dear Mr. Chairman:

On behalf of the international delegation organized by the National Democratic Institute, I want to thank you for the very informative and productive meeting today in your office at the Supreme Election Committee.

As we said during the meeting, it is our impression after a brief introduction to your country, that the electoral system being put in place in Yemen is consistent with international standards. Of course, time will tell whether it continues as well as it has begun, but the process clearly has begun well. Your considerable personal experience in the organization of previous elections is quite evident, and explains why Yemen is now the leader in the Arab world in the field of genuine elections.

Your invitation to the international community to send observers is much welcomed. You may expect that NDI, in cooperation with its Republican counterpart, will endeavor to organize a multi-national delegation to be present at the time of the April 27 elections. As we discussed, an international monitoring program would necessarily require additional pre-election missions between now and the election date, possibly one small delegation in late February and another in March, to be followed by a larger delegation at the time of the April elections.

Equally heartening to us was your readiness to accommodate domestic Yemeni election observers, even though the law is silent on this point. As in many other countries, the Election Committee may in this case authorize responsible independent groups to support the election process by granting them access to the voting and counting centers. You will recall that Thomas Melia, Program Director at the NDI, indicated that his organization has considerable experience in providing technical assistance and training to such groups to ensure that they operate in a genuinely nonpartisan and professional manner. We were all very pleased that you invited the NDI to provide such assistance in Yemen. NDI will plan to respond positively to any such requests it receives.

As you know, the International Foundation for Electoral Systems (IFES) based in the U.S., and the Electoral Reform Society (ERS), based in Britain, are prepared to offer various technical assistance and commodities to the Supreme Election Committee as you deem appropriate. These are both quite efficient and highly regarded organizations and can be relied upon.

Once again, I thank you for your hospitality today. I hope to see you again soon.

Yours sincerely,

John Bruton
Member of Parliament
Leader of the Parliamentary Opposition
Ireland

*Appendix V*

# Letter from YODRL to NDI
# Announcing Formation of NCFE

THE YEMENI ORGANIZATION FOR THE DEFENSE
OF RIGHTS AND LIBERTIES (YODRL)
Sana'a, Yemen Republic

No       :
Date    : Feb. 1st, 1993
Encl.   :

---

NATIONAL DEMOCRATIC INSTITUTE
FOR INTERNATIONAL AFFAIRS
MR. THOMAS O. MELIA
PROGRAM DIRECTOR

Dear Sir,

We have the pleasure to inform you that the YEMEN ORGANIZATION FOR THE DEFENSE OF RIGHTS AND LIBERTIES (YODRL) has formed a NATIONAL COMMITTEE FOR FREE ELECTIONS (NCFE). This committee is a non-governmental and unbiased group with the only goal of consolidating the democratic procedures taking place these days in Yemen and also guaranteeing free and clean elections. This goal will be through ensuring the legal procedures, informing the citizens about their constitutional rights in participating in all the different steps of the elections, and also making sure of the electoral procedures.

Since the government and the Supreme Committee for Elections have publicly announced their welcome to all foreign organizations willing to participate in the supervision of the first democratic elections in Yemen without reservations and according to our previous meetings in Sana'a and Aden, YODRL warmly welcomes establishing mutual cooperation between NDIIA and NCFE to help your institute watching the elections.

Meanwhile your institute is requested to provide NCFE with the necessary and needed training and possible financial assistance for the teams to be required under NCFE supervision. YODRL will provide premises for the activities of this mission within the limits of its poor financial means.

Mr. MUSTAPHA A.M. NOMAN the member of the supreme council of YODRL will preside NCFE and take the responsibility of coordinating with your institute.

YODRL will do all the necessary efforts to mass the political parties efforts to support and cooperate with NCFE with the full commitment of independency and neutrality.

Looking forward to receive your reply, and wishing you a pleasant journey back home.

Dr. Mohamed A. MALIK AL-MUTAWKIL
Vice-President YORDL

*Appendix VI*

# Letter from NDI to SEC About Working with NCFE

February 2, 1993

Al-Qadi Abdul Karim Al-Arashi
Member, Presidential Council
Chairman, Supreme Election Committee
Sana'a, Republic of Yemen

Dear Mr. Chairman:

Further to the letter dated January 31, 1993, addressed to you by Mr. John Bruton, I would like also to express my personal appreciation for the hospitality you extended to our delegation on Sunday. I realize full well the many demands on your time in these weeks preceding the April 27 elections, and I am extremely grateful that you spent so much time with our multi-national delegation.

I would also like to inform you that the National Democratic Institute has received a request from the newly formed National Committee for Free Elections. Consistent with your statement to the delegation, it is our intention to respond positively to this request. The president of the executive committee of the National Committee for Free Elections is Mr. Mustapha A. Noman. He and several colleagues are presently gathering a council of advisors, including representatives of all parties and numerous independent personalities. I am persuaded that Mr. Noman's intention is to mobilize support for free and genuine elections in Yemen, and that they will cooperate fully with the Supreme Election Committee.

I expect that NDI will organize a first training program for the Committee later in February.  I hope that we can work with the SEC Technical Committee to ensure that the work of the National Committee for Free Elections is consistent with the electoral law and the decisions of the SEC.

Very truly yours,

Thomas O. Melia
Program Director

*Appendix VII*

# Letter from NDI to
# Foreign Minister Al-Eryani

February 5, 1993

Dr. Abdul Karim Al-Eryani
Minister of Foreign Affairs
Sana'a, Republic of Yemen

Dear Dr. Al-Eryani:

I want to thank you for your assistance during NDI's recent visit to Yemen. Your support has been invaluable, both during the preparation stages for the mission, as well as during the week spent meeting with officials in Sana'a and Aden.

Thank you also for taking the time to meet with us on Monday, February 1. Hearing your views regarding the upcoming April elections provided useful insights into the Yemeni political process currently underway.

Since returning home, I have had several conversations with Mustapha A. Noman, who is chairman of the newly formed National Committee for Free Elections. I gather that the project has already stumbled a bit since I left, in that Mr. Noman and the chairman of the Supreme Election Committee do not see eye to eye about the utility of independent observers. I do not think it appropriate that an outsider such as myself should try to play the role of mediator. But I will continue to try to advise Mustapha Noman on ways he can cooperate with the SEC.

Especially after my visit to the Operations Center of the SEC, I think the role of the NCFE should be to work closely with the SEC. Moreover, I believe that public (and international) confidence in the organizational abilities of the SEC would be enhanced by providing informal access to leaders of opposition parties, journalists and diplomats.

I gather from Mr. Noman that there is some question about the precise scope of the Committee's work, and its access to certain kinds of information. As far as I can discern from afar, the differences of view on this point are not sufficiently large that they should pose any obstacle to moving ahead with the project. So I am encouraging Mr. Noman to proceed, confident that differences can be resolved in good faith as we proceed.

As you suggested, I will work with John Babb to prepare a letter for future visits.

I look forward to seeing you again.

Yours sincerely,

Thomas O. Melia
Program Director

*Appendix VIII*

# Text of Article in *The Elections* Concerning Supreme Election Commission (SEC) Approval of the National Committee for Free Elections (NCFE)

## *The Elections* (Week of February 14, 1993)

### "Approving Elections Monitoring in Accordance with the Regulations and Rules of the Law"

The High Commission for the Elections has received requests from the National Committee for Free Elections and the Yemeni Organization for the Defense of Rights and Liberties to allow the presence of representatives from the two organizations at the ballot centers to observe the voting process and guarantee honesty.

The Commission received a letter from Thomas Melia, the Program Director of the National Democratic Institute, informing the Chairman of the Higher Commission Judge Abd al-Karim al-Arashi that the Institute has received a request from the National Committee for Free Elections to organize training sessions for Yemeni volunteers.   Mr. Melia intends to answer him positively, and expressed his pleasure for Yemen's welcome and willingness to receive international observers for the elections.

*The Elections* learned that the High Commission reviewed during its meetings this week the requests for local and international monitoring teams, and accepted them in principle.  The regulations, conditions and rules for this process will be organized in accordance with the activity of the Commission and in coordination with the recognized and organized political parties.  This monitoring should not affect the freedom and honesty of the elections nor under any circumstances turn into a means of influence.

*Appendix IX*

# Translations of Articles on Morocco Trip by Hisham Bashraheel

## *Al-Ayyam*, vol. 12, no. 128, April 28, 1993

### "With the NDI Team in Morocco (1/3): The Yemeni Hopes for a Democracy That is not for Export, While the Moroccan Desires a Democracy That is not Cosmetic"

The issue of democracy in many Third World countries, including the Arab world and Yemen, is still the focus of lengthy discussions. Seemingly, these discussions are characterized by seriousness, [concern for] the national interest and for a desire to catch up with the culture of the nations that preceded us in democratization. In reality, however, they are a manifestation of political luxury and [the need] of the regimes of these [Arab] states, either the ruling or the opposition parties as well as some politicians, to avoid being accused of totalitarianism with respect to their thought or policies. This takes place at a time when the fortresses, systems and symbols of totalitarianism have already collapsed. This is also an imperative result of superior divine and international trickles [impact] on the backward conditions of these countries and their governments − and what they inflicted upon their people − that remained isolated for a long time because of the cold war between the West and the East.

Some of the countries and parties, that have already been existing or those which revived their activities, that have recently adopted democracy refuse to uphold the correct fundamentals of democracy. They try to distort and adapt [manipulate] it to suit only their interests. They are similar to a baby who refuses to take his medicine and food to overcome his chronic disease and prolong his life. Fooling around with democracy in these countries is indeed a distortion and degeneration of its noble and great meanings for which people have struggled and offered scores of martyrs.

The preparations for all the phases of the first free elections in our country after the unification and the adoption of a multiparty system for the first time in Yemen; the discussions that accompanied the elections, and my selection by the NDI — to which I am thankful — to participate with a team that monitored democracy, freedom and human rights in Morocco have all enabled me to understand many details regarding the process of democratization in the two countries (Yemen and Morocco) and the loopholes in some of the processes that contradict the correct understanding of democracy.

There are similarities between Yemen and Morocco, especially in the political process and in granting freedom following the adoption of pluralism. Yet the differences that I saw certainly testify in favor of the democratic process and freedom in Yemen. With regards to the condition of human rights, the situation in Yemen cannot be compared to that in Morocco, mainly because of the violations to which some brothers in the Moroccan opposition are exposed. This was confirmed by the reports of the International Organization of Human Rights and by Amnesty International. In this respect, there are two human rights organizations in Yemen and Morocco. In Morocco, the monitoring team of the NDI, of which I was a member, paid a visit to the Advisory Commission for Human Rights, which has been formed by the state to provide its views to the king and the state on what it considered as violations of human rights. A heated discussion took place between the members of the team and the members of the presidency of the Commission about violations of human rights in Morocco. I asked the members of the Commission about the party that violates human rights the most. One member answered: the Ministry of the Interior and [the Ministry of] Justice. The rest of the members became quickly alert and added: this is his personal opinion.

I was astonished by the tremendous structure and modern furnishings of the Commission building, which is considered one of the landmarks in Rabat and was previously occupied by the League of Arab States.

In Casablanca, the team met a member of the Moroccan Organization for Human Rights which is independent from the state and the majority of its members are former political detainees. This Moroccan brother told me that there are those who became dumb and others became permanently handicapped as a result of torture. Those who were lucky were released but stayed unemployed even though they held university degrees. This situation and this violation of human rights reminds us of the conditions in Yemen before the unification, particularly in South Yemen and what used to take place of torture, chasing and banishment.

With regards to the freedom of expression through the mass media, the two countries are similar. There are party newspapers as well as independent ones. However, they are ineffective because they do represent a means of communication with the majority of the people. This is attributed to the spread of illiteracy and the presence of a large number of official newspapers and others that belong to the ruling parties. The printed papers and magazines do not reflect the true meanings of democracy as they offer at best 10% of the opposing point of view, constructive criticism and links with the citizens.

Radio and television, on the other hand, which provide 95% and 65 percent of communications, respectively, constitute the two most successful links with the majority of the citizens. They are still however under the control of the state in Yemen and Morocco. This contradicts the process of democratization in the two countries. In all the democratic nations, there is not a ministry of information — except for the Third World countries and the Arab World — or state owned newspapers, nor this large number of ruling party papers, as is the case in Yemen and Morocco.

The two countries are similar with respect to a law which contradicts democracy. [This law] prohibits criticizing the head of the state — the king or the president. It is not enforced in Yemen though, as some papers and writers have criticized — in respect and with restraint — the head of the state without any legal action being taken against them. The presence of this law, nonetheless, is a flaw in any system claiming to be democratic.

In one of the meetings that took place at the office of *Al-Ayyam* between a member of the Republican Institute, which coordinates the reception of foreign delegation monitoring the elections, and a group of intellectuals, a brother made a comment which drew my attention. He told the member of the Republican Institute that he hoped that the Yemeni democracy would not be for export, explaining that it should not be [used] for the purpose of giving a positive image to the outside, while it is not actually practiced inside. In Morocco, the General Secretary of the Moroccan Workers Federation Mahjoub Bin Siddiq told the NDI team that he hoped that democracy in Morocco would not be only cosmetic.

*Al-Ayyam,* vol. 12, no. 129, May 3, 1993

**"With the NDI Team in Morocco (2/3): The Yemeni Hopes for a Democracy That is not for Export, While the Moroccan Desires a Democracy That is not Cosmetic: The Minister of the Interior and Information Received us in the Longest Meeting that Lasted for Only 90 Seconds"**

On the road of democratization and pluralism, it is worth noting that Morocco has begun its democratization process with more positive steps than Yemen. Morocco is currently preparing to hold parliamentary elections scheduled to take place next June. These elections were preceded by the municipal elections. This process did not take place in Yemen despite demands for holding municipal elections before the parliamentary elections. Moreover, the system of the local municipalities reminds me of the status of the municipality of Aden that was established in 1888. In this regard, the Moroccan system is a replica of the system of Aden before and after independence, before the hands (forces) of destruction worked on diluting and eliminating its role. The municipalities in Morocco enjoy complete financial and administrative independence. Their affairs are run by a municipal council that is elected by the citizens. The council in turn elects a president from amongst its members.

I visited with the NDI team the municipality of Dar Bouazzah, which has a population of 70,000 people and is 30 kilometers far from Casablanca. We were received by the president and members of the *jamaa*, a Moroccan term for the municipality. The president of the *jamaa* Brother Ali Belhaj is a learned young man who received his education in the United States. He informed the team about the projects of the municipality of Dar Bouazzah, mainly housing and commercial projects, which have already been implemented. He also showed us a completed plan for a hospital for which the municipality is currently preparing studies and will cost $10 million. The municipality will finance this project which is considered the first of a kind in Morocco.

Brother Ali Belhaj, the president of a 25-member group, explained to me that the revenues of the municipality are raised from all kinds of local tax such as housing construction, sale and purchase tax, cleaning and sewage, commercial license, etc. Regarding employment in Dar Bouazzah, he mentioned that employment takes place on the basis that it is considered a part of the responsibilities of the *jamaa*.

The results of the municipal elections demonstrate the extent of the popularity of the major political parties in Morocco.  The Rassemblement National des Independents won 4,500 seats; Union Constitutionnelle 2,900; Istiqlal 2,750; Mouvement Populaire 2,680.  Some parties, however, criticized many of the election processes such as transferring scores of citizens from one region to another for voting purposes, and eventually for changing the outcome.  The same issue was a point of complaint by many candidates in the general parliamentary elections in Yemen, particularly with regards to the issue of the [military] barracks.  This complaint does not mean, at any rate, depriving the members of the armed forces of their legitimate right of voting as citizens.  However, [it aims at putting an end to] the way by which the voting process was handled and manipulated in favor of one candidate over another.  The members of the armed forces should have cast their votes in their barracks to the candidates of their districts of origin.

While monitoring the elections in Morocco, we visited all political parties, ruling and opposition, as well as the labor unions.  One of the negative aspects of political pluralism in Morocco is that it was reflected on the labor unions and split their ranks.  Whereas Morocco in the past used to have one labor union for all the workers of the country, it now has more than one union, each belonging to a specific political party.  The old General Union, headed by Mahjoub Bin Siddiq, remained independent of any political party.  It is the General Union for Independence.

During his talk with the team, Bin Siddiq, who coined the expression "we hope our democracy is not cosmetic," mentioned that the politicization of the unions does not serve the interests of the working classes.  The other labor union, which is headed by Abdel Razzaq Afilal does not represent at best more than 150,000 workers, whereas our union represents between 450,000 and 550,000 workers.  Bin Siddiq asserted that before participating in the parliamentary elections, many reforms should be taken in order to protect the interests of the workers and the benefits which they managed to achieve over several years. These interests are now being threatened.  Unless such reforms are undertaken, we are not going to participate in the next elections.

In a meeting with one of the opposition parties, Union Socialiste des Forces Populaires, Abdel Rahman al-Youssifi, the Secretary General, said that for 30 years his party has been struggling in the opposition for democracy and the implementation of the law. His comments on the municipal elections are that the officials at the election centers were all policemen, who follow the orders of the state and work according to its will. He also noted that drug trade and corruption played a role in the municipal elections. He warned that this might be repeated in the parliamentary elections. He added that "we need to avoid the mistakes that took place in the municipal elections by standardizing registration, because many voters were able to cast their votes without having registration cards. In addition, we must apply secret ink [stamp] on the fingers of the voters so that they could not cast their votes many times over." This suggestion is rejected by the official authorities on the basis that it would offend the Moroccan citizen.

Before discussing the topic of the last article which deals with the political parties and the constitution in Morocco, it is worth mentioning that there is a consensus on the leadership and legitimacy of King Hassan.

I was very much surprised by what I heard from the leaders of the Parti du Progres et du Socialisme, formerly the members of the Communist Party, regarding this issue. As the saying goes, they are more royalist than the king. I would like also to take this opportunity to refer to the team's meeting with Brother Idris al-Basri, the Minister of the Interior and Information, who received us in one of the longest meetings of the team in Morocco that lasted for only 90 seconds. We will deal with these issues in more details next week. God Willing.

### *Al-Ayyam,* vol. 12, no. 131, May 19, 1993

**"With the NDI Team in Morocco (3/3): "The Minister of the Interior and Information Received us in the Longest Meeting that Lasted for only 90 Seconds"**

During the team's meeting with Brother Idris al-Basri, the Minister of the Interior and Information, we were received by the director of his office at the Ministry of the Interior. After the introduction, al-Basri called for his advisors, who were three. The minister pointed and immediately TV cameras were taking shots of the team. After they finished, the minister apologized for not being able to continue meeting with us, requesting that we carry on the meeting with his advisors. Thus our meeting with the minister lasted for only 90 seconds.

I sat next to one of the advisors. I was later told that his son was married to one of King Hassan's daughters. A conversation was raised about democracy, wider political participation and human rights. During the conversation, I requested the team's permission to conduct it in Arabic with the advisors. I said that King Hassan with his leadership of the Moroccan regime was able to withstand firmly many of the severe storms that blew over his country and the Arab world. However, the international changes and the democratic wind which is storming many of the countries of the world today require some changes in Morocco in order to preserve the [continuity] of King Hassan as a symbol for the Moroccan people. King Hassan is considered as one of the shrewdest Arab leaders and he cannot be overlooking these changes. And you [the advisors] around him should contribute in expanding the prospects for the political participation for every Moroccan.

I was surprised that their reply to me was conducted in French. I then asked to take the chance to translate what I said earlier to the rest of the members of the team. The conversation in the Ministry of the Interior lasted 90 minutes.

During the team's meeting with a number of ruling and opposition parties, I noticed the absence of young elements in the leadership of all the Moroccan political parties. All the members of the present leadership are senior and old politicians who have been rotating for decades in assuming ministerial positions without giving opportunities to the young elements. This, in my view, does not serve the political process in Morocco. To some extent, the same situation applies to Yemen. The Moroccan political parties, nonetheless, are different from Yemen's in another respect. The Moroccan political parties are older, more deep-rooted and have larger followings of the Moroccan people than some Yemeni political parties whose number of followers does not exceed that of the members of one family, and at best cases, their number will not be greater than that of a village. Some might justify this phenomenon by referring to the large difference in the number of the populations of the two countries. But the fact is that this phenomenon exists.

*Appendix X*

# NCFE Statistics on Participants in March Training Conferences

16 March 1993

**Table 1. Beneficiaries of NDI-NCFE's Training Conferences conducted at several governorates of Yemen in the period 9-15 March 1993**

| Center & Date | Total of Trainees | Partisans | Non-partisans | Did not state | Males | Females |
|---|---|---|---|---|---|---|
| Sana'a 9-3 | 136 | 10 | 90 | 36 | 129 | 7 |
| Aden 10-3 | 70 | 14 | 41 | 15 | 51 | 19 |
| Taiz 11-3 | 51 | 6 | 45 | 10 | 42 | 9 |
| Hudaid 13-3 | 130 | 54 | 54 | 22 | 74 | 56 |
| Dhamar 13-3 | 55 | 15 | 10 | 30 | 55 | |
| Sana'a For Partisans 14-3 | 37 | 37 | | | 35 | 2 |
| Haja 15-3 | 114 | 32 | 69 | 13 | 114 | |
| Total | 593 | 168 | 309 | 126 | 500 | 93 |

*Editor's Note: numerical inconsistencies attributable to original document.*

16 March 1993

**Table 2. Partisans Attended NDI-NCFE's Training Conferences 9-15 March 1993**

| Center | A | B | C | D | E | F | G | H | I | J | K | L | M | N |
|--------|---|---|---|---|---|---|---|---|---|---|---|---|---|---|
| Sana'a | | 4 | 3 | 1 | 1 | | 1 | | | | | | | |
| Aden | 6 | 1 | 1 | 1 | 4 | 2 | | | | | | | | |
| Tai'z | 1 | | | | 2 | | | | | | | | | 3 |
| al-Hudaidah | 3 | 1 | 4 | 6 | 38 | | | | | | | 2 | | |
| Dhamar | 2 | 1 | 4 | 1 | 7 | | 1 | | | | | | 1 | |
| Sana'a for Partisans | | | | 14 | 2 | | | | 6 | 8 | 5 | 2 | | |
| Haja | 2 | 4 | 1 | 9 | 7 | 1 | | | | | | | 8 | |
| Total | 14 | 11 | 13 | 32 | 61 | 3 | 2 | | 6 | 8 | 5 | 4 | 9 | 3 |

A = Yemeni Socialist Party
B = Hizb al-k-Ba'th al-'Arabial-Ishtiraki
C = Hizb al-Tashih al-Nasiri / noon
D = Al-Tajamu al-Yamani lil-Islah
E = People's General Congress
F = Rabitat Abna al-Yaman
G = Itihad al-Quwa al-Sha'biyah
H = Al-Jabhah al-Wataniyah / nom
I = Hizb al-Haq
J = Itihad al-Quwa al-Thawriyah
K = Al-Hizb al-Wahdawi al-Nasiri
L = Al-Tajamu' al-Wahdawi al-Yamani
M = Partisan
N = Hizb al-Ahrar al-Dusturi

*Appendix XI*

# NCFE Statement of Purpose and Training Documents

20 April 1993

The National Committee for Free Elections (NCFE) was founded in January of 1993 for the purpose of organizing and training Yemeni citizens to take an active and personal role in ensuring that our first free, multiparty elections are conducted in a fair and honest manner. We hope to accomplish this purpose by planning a project of election observation by Yemeni citizens.

NCFE sought the participation and input of all political parties, the current government, the Supreme Election Committee (SEC) and the international community in our efforts to guarantee that our domestic observation project would be supported by all Yemeni citizens while maintaining an attitude of strict non-partisan impartiality. An Advisory Council was established comprised of political parties, business people, academics and prominent personalities. These individuals have been kept informed of our activities and have supported the plans of the Committee. The execution of this project is the responsibility of a executive committee made up of non-partisan Yemeni volunteers.

Rather than advocating any particular election results, our aim is to provide Yemeni citizens with an honest and impartial opinion about the fairness of the elections.

The National Democratic Institute (NDI) responded to NCFE's request for assistance in the planning of this project, the first of its kind in the Arab world. NDI is providing some financial support as well as continuing advice based on its experiences working in dozens of emerging democracies during the last decade.

NCFE and NDI received initial support and approval from the SEC and from Yemenis of all political persuasions. Unfortunately, the SEC has retreated from its approval during the last several weeks. NCFE has, however, continued to recruit and train thousands of Yemeni citizens. The enthusiasm, courage and dedication that has arisen in response to the NCFE project has been remarkable.

Yemenis have made it clear that they want democracy and they want the guarantee of fairness that can only come from being allowed to observe the process first hand.

We expect upwards of 4,000 citizens volunteering in these observation efforts on election day, beginning a new tradition of civic involvement by average citizens. Our efforts will also serve to compliment and enhance similar observation projects of the international community and the SEC.

If the SEC continues to block domestic observation efforts, our volunteers will still arrive at the polling stations on election day. They will create no disturbances at the polling sites, but will observe as much of the process as possible while they vote themselves, and they will interview voters as they leave the polling sites.

Our domestic observation project will be severely compromised by the refusal of the authorities to give us access, but we will succeed in planting a seed for the growth of civic organizations and active citizen participation in our new democracy.

## The National Committee for Free Elections

### Instruction and Information For Election Observers

27 April 1993

Q. Who is an observer and what is his or her role?

A. An election observer is a member of the National Committee for Free Elections (NCFE), who has volunteered for this activity in one of the constituencies and has taken an oath before the governorate coordinator. His or her role is limited to observing all procedures that take place on electoral day, Tuesday, 27th April 1993, and to record his or her observations in the NCFE supplied form. The observer has no right to interfere in the duties of the election committee, either by advice or by agreeing to (or objecting to) any measure taken by the committee, regardless of whether or not such measures is in accordance with the election law and the instructions of the Supreme Election Committee (SEC). The observer has no right to interfere with the representatives of the parties, the candidates or their representatives, by either advice or objection.

Q. What are the actions that should be taken by the observer on election day?

A. The actions of the observer should be as follows:

First: On the morning of election day, before the casting of votes:

1. The observer should have equipped himself or herself with everything needed for the observation process, including:

    a. The NCFE supplied permit, which gives the observer the right to enter all constituency centers for monitoring. This permit will be given to the observer by the NCFE governorate coordinator.

    b. The observer should have all NCFE forms and papers which he or she shall use in these activities.

    c. The observer should introduce himself or herself to the chairman of the election committee at the constituency of the voting center.

2. The election observer should arrive at the voting center at which he or she has volunteered at 7 a.m. to do the following:

a.   Introduce himself or herself by showing the NCFE permit to observe the election to the chairman of the election committee at the constituency or the voting center.

b.   Generally review the place at which the casting of votes will occur.

c.   Record the number of registered votes from the "Register of Voters," on the relevant form.

d.   Record the names of candidates at the constituency on the said form.

e.   Be present at the constituency or voting center to observe the opening of the box or boxes by the chairman and members of the election committee in front of all present voters, candidates or their representative, so that they are sure that the boxes are empty before voting begins. The observer should observe the election committee during the writing of the relevant report for that occasion, and he or she should note the placement of the boxes in the center.

Second:   During the voting process 8 a.m. to 6 p.m. as follows:

1.   After completing the previous steps, the casting of votes will start at 8 a.m. and the role of the observer will be:

a.   To observe the process of casting votes and to observe the chairman of the election committee when he or she compares the voters' registration cards with the register of voters at the center; to observe as each voter is given the voting card; to observe when voters cast their votes behind the screen in full secrecy; and to observe voters when they insert their voting cards in the box. During the whole process no one present has any right to influence the free choice of any voter by saying or doing anything, so long as voters can read and write. If a voter is illiterate, and there are no mean to enable him or her to mark a voting card, the voter may asks for help in marking a voting card from any other voter he or she trusts or to ask for help from the chairman of the election committee. The voter should insert his or her voting card in the box unassisted. The observer should note when the election committee checks off the names of voters who have already cast their voters, and to observe the voters as they put the "election" ink on their left thumb, so that voters cannot cast votes again.

b.  The observer should continue his or her activities until the end of the election day (6 p.m. if there are no voters at the voting center and 8 p.m. if the voters continue to arrive), when the chairman of the election committee declares the end of the casting of votes. If the observer notices the occurrence of any problems that might influence the result of the election at any time during the election day, he or she should report it to the area or governorate coordinator through the NCFE "roving" observers. If the observer cannot find one of them, he or she can get help of a voter or a party or candidate representative to contact the coordinator and ask for his or her help.

c.  The observer should continue to monitor the procedures after the conclusion of vote casting; when the election committee waxes and stamps all the openings of the boxes and writes the relevant report which should be signed by all members of the election committee and the candidate or their representatives; and when the whole committee moves to the main voting center; and when the counting committee is formed from all members of the election committees in that constituency; and when this committee checks the adequacy of the wax and stamps and locks on all boxes. All these measures should be taken in the presence of the candidates or their representatives. A report should be written and signed on this occasion by the counting committee. The counting committee should then begin the counting process – counting the votes in each box separately. The vote results for every candidate should be copied to a list which contains the name of every candidate. The head of the counting committee should put a mark on every voting card counted and should mark it with the number of the box it was in. The cards favoring each candidate should be gathered in a bundle. This process continues when the number of votes should be copied into a cumulative list which shows the total correct votes which were gained by every candidate. The candidate who gains the highest number of votes should be declared the winning candidate, concluding the election process.

Third:

With the declaration of election results, the election process ends. The role of the observer also comes to an end, as related to the elections for the new parliament. At this moment the NCFE observer should finish recording all that he or she has noticed from the beginning of the process until the declaration of the winning candidate. The observer should emphasize that his or her role started and finished without any kind of interference from the observer in all the activities during the day, whether they were according to election laws or not. The observer should testify that what he or she wrote on the form is what he or she has seen personally and not what was reported to the observer. In this case the observer will have accomplished what he or she volunteered for in a true and honest way. He should surrender the NCFE for, after completing and signing the form, to the NCFE governance coordinator.

Important notice for the observer:

In case you are not allowed to stay inside the polling station to do your duty as an observer, do the following:

1.  Leave the polling station. Do not object or refuse to follow the orders of the election officials.

2.  Record on your form that you were ordered to leave.

3.  Record on your form all observations you were able to make during the time you are inside the polling station voting yourself.

4.  Stand outside to the polling station and interview voters as they are leaving. Record their responses on the form supplied by NCFE.

## NCFE Voting Center Observer Form

27 April 1993

1.  Were the ballot booths arranged to ensure the secrecy of voters?
2.  Level of security men's presence:   none   light   heavy
3.  Average time waiting to vote:   long   suitable
4.  Percent of voters who used more than average:
    20-40%   50-70%   more than normal
5.  How was the situation outside the ballot station?
    organized   not organized
6.  Presence of registration forms of those who were allowed to
    vote:   100%   80%   60%
7.  Percent of voters allowed to vote with I.D. cards:
    20%   40%   less
8.  Percent of illiterate voters or blind:   90%   70%   40%   less
9.  Absence of committee members:   many   few   never
10. Did the committee stop any citizen from voting?   yes   no
11. How was the level of citizens interest to vote?
    morning   noon   end of day   (high, average, low)
12. How was the behavior of the committee members with the
    voters?
    good   bad
13. Was the location of ballot center in a heavy or unpopulated
    district?
14. Was the location far from the populated area?   yes   no

General Questions on the Counting Process:

1.  Did the counting committee ensure the condition of the boxes
    upon arrival from ballot centers before opening them to count?
    yes   no
2.  When did the counting committee open the first box?
    as soon as boxes arrived   at a later time
3.  Did the counting committee open the boxes individually?
    yes   no
4.  Were the contents of each box counted separately?   yes   no
5.  Were the ballots marked with a box number?   And were they
    returned to the same box?   yes   no
6.  Were the ballots of each candidate gathered in a bundle form?
    yes   no

7. Were the ballots marked after the information was copied to the special form of votes for each candidate? yes  no

8. Was there a dispute over the illegal votes? yes  no
   If yes, what caused the dispute and how was it settled?

9. Was the situation quiet before and during the counting process? yes  no
   If no, please specify:
   light noises  average  disturbance  fighting

10. When was the counting finished?
    the same day  the following day

11. Were the results announced immediately? yes  no

12. Was the winner's name announced by the counting committee? yes  no

13. What was the candidate's and the representative's reaction after the announcement of the results? satisfied  not satisfied  both

14. What was the voters' reaction?
    satisfied  not satisfied  both

15. How was the performance level of the counting committee and their behavior with the candidates? good  average  bad

We certify the above on behalf of NCFE

Observers' names:

Signatures:

Candidates' or representatives' names: (optional)

## NCFE Counting Center Observer Form

27 April 1993

Name and number of constituency:
Number of ballot center:
Number of boxes:
Serial number of boxes:
Name of NCFE observer:
Names of election committee officials:
Names of candidates or representatives:
Were you present when boxes arrived? yes no
Were the boxes opened before the voting process? yes no
Were the boxes put in a visible location? yes no
Were all of the necessary items for voting available? (List of voters, voting cards, ink, curtains and a poster of the candidates names)
Total number of voters in the center:
Total number of cards before the voting process started:
Total number of security men present:
Did the voting start at 8 a.m.? yes no
If "no" specify the time:
Number of people who voted:
Number of people prohibited from voting:
Number of cards canceled or destroyed:
Number of remaining cards at the end of the day:
Time of closing:
Were the boxes locked and waxed properly? yes no
Names of the persons who accompanied the boxes to the counting center and their relationship to the voting process:
Were all of these persons in one car with the boxes? yes no
Time of transferring the boxes to the counting center:
Did you accompany the boxes? yes no
Were the boxes opened before arriving at the counting center?

Observer's Name:
Signature:
Comments:
1. Any details on the above
2. Registering any details concerning the voting process not mentioned before

*Appendix XII*

# Letter from NCFE to SEC Reiterating Request for Permission to Monitor Elections

In the Name of God, the Merciful, the Compassionate

Republic of Yemen
National Committee                11 Shawwal 1413 A.H.
For Free Elections                April 3, 1992
    (NCFE)

Distinguished brothers, the honorable Chairman, Vice Chairman, and members of the Supreme Election Committee:

The National Committee for Free Elections sends you its regards and wishes on this occasion to remind you of the request submitted to your venerable committee on February 6, 1993, to obtain the necessary permission for National Committee volunteers to undertake domestic monitoring of the parliamentary elections on April 27. Your committee discussed the request on February 14, 1993, approved it, and forwarded it to the chairman of the legal committee for the committee to formulate guidelines as it saw fit to achieve this end.

In this regard, we would like to present to your venerable committee a brief summary of the goals and tasks of the NCFE, its membership, its activities as of the date of this memorandum, its relationships with the parties and the candidates, and its constitutional and legal status, as follows:

## I.   Membership of the NCFE:

The NCFE is composed of independent individuals who do not belong to any political party or organization.

The NCFE consists of two bodies:

### Executive body

All members of the executive body are qualified independents who are not candidates. Their tasks are to determine how monitoring will proceed, recruit and train volunteers, coordinate with entities concerned with the elections, and implement monitoring plans and procedures.

### Consultative body

The consultative body includes nationally-known members of the society and representatives of political parties and organizations. Their task is to assist the executive body by overcoming difficulties it may face in implementing its tasks, to provide it with information, and to observe the procedures implemented by the executive committee, without interfering with its practices or procedures.

## II.  Goals of the NCFE:

Among the most important goals of the NCFE are: to provide a reliable guarantee of impartial, free elections through neutral, popular monitoring of the upcoming parliamentary elections; to seek to establish a national heritage in order to improve the democratic process by observing errors and negative aspects and striving to eliminate them in the future; and to strengthen the credibility of the democratic trend both at home and abroad.  When performing the tasks for which it was formed, the Committee is bound by the constitution and the laws of the country.  The fact that it is not affiliated with any organization or party does not mean that it has no relationship with political parties or organizations.  Its organizational structure includes a consultative body made up of parties, organizations, and prominent members of the society.  The task of this body is to cooperate with the executive committee to overcome difficulties that may impede its work; to provide all necessary facilities so that the committee can do its work; to provide information, data, documents, and records related to the committee's tasks and operations.  Thus political parties and organizations play a consultative, cooperative role in the NCFE.  The NCFE makes its own decisions in all its activities.  It is for this reason that its organizational structure requires that there be a consultative body that includes a representative of every political party or organization as well as nationally-known members of the society concerned with this issue.

## III.  Tasks and Activities of the NCFE:

In accordance with the goals of the NCFE, while it is carrying out its work it is bound by the constitution and the laws in effect and can in no way exceed or violate them; instead, it will be the first to be concerned with implementing and abiding by them. The NCFE is not interested in correcting violations, protesting violations, providing advice, or interfering in the work of the Supreme Election Committee or its committees, etc. The role of the Committee is merely to monitor and observe. For this reason, the essential requirement for members of the NCFE, coordinators in the governorates, and volunteers is that they be independent and not be members of any political party or organization. In order to ensure that this condition is met, an oath has been prepared for every volunteer who wishes to work with the Committee, and every volunteer signs a form warranting that he is not a member of any political party or organization. So that the NCFE can operate with complete independence and impartiality, work with the Committee is voluntary and is not compensated. The Committee does not rely on any entity for financial support for its operations, but does accept unconditional grants, cooperation, and donations.

## IV. Importance of the NCFE and its Work:

The preceding shows the importance of the NCFE. By virtue of the condition imposed on its members and of its goals and tasks, it does not represent any entity or interest involved in the elections. The significance of its existence and its work lies in its neutrality and independence. The Elections Law guarantees each candidate a presence in the election room, thus guaranteeing the private right of the candidate to ensure that proper procedures are followed and results are correct. The Law provides the candidate a basis for personal and private assurance. His monitoring virtually administers a presence with his personal interests. This clearly shows the importance of fulfilling the legal dimension of the question of monitoring as it relates to the general welfare and the interest of the society through the presence of the NCFE, which is concerned with monitoring on behalf of society, providing confidence, and arbitrating and settling disputes. Its existence derives from the *sharia* (eliminating the sources of corruption takes precedence over bringing about good). The work of the NCFE can help eliminate the sources of corruption and bring about good for society. Whoever represents his own interest cannot monitor his own activity because man cannot be a witness for himself; the witness must be another.

It is well known that anyone who loses an election causes an outcry, spreading rumors and defamation. He uses every means, including his sympathizers, to influence public opinion about the soundness of procedures, activities, and results. He raises doubts and suspicions among the citizens about all that transpired as a reaction to not achieving his personal interests. For this reason, the NCFE was created. In keeping with the above, with its neutrality, and with its volunteer, popular nature, the NCFE's impartial report will be important to refute accusations and remarks that arise about the elections. It will enable the nation and its citizens to avoid confusion, vituperation, and dissention, God forbid, for we have had enough of this in the past. While the NCFE pursues its honorable, noble task, it is ensuring the health of the country's democratic process in the eyes of its citizens and concerned persons outside the country. We do not intend raise fears or to spread confusion by monitoring the elections.

Popular, specialized monitoring can be a hallmark of democracy. It is not an innovation devised in our country; in fact, similar organizations exist in many sister, friendly, and other countries throughout the world. Such organizations are considered a sign of a reliable guarantee of free, impartial elections.

## V. Constitutional and Legal Status of the NCFE:

With reference to Law No. 41 of 1992, we do not find any stipulation preventing domestic or international monitoring of elections. Nor do we find any stipulation allowing such monitoring.

Civil Law No. 19 of 1992, which is an essential authority for all laws, states in Article 3: "Islamic *sharia* is based on protection of the interests of the people and elimination of the causes of corruption."

Article 4 states: "...eliminating the sources of corruption takes precedence over bringing about good when the two are incompatible..."

Article 11 states: "Clearly established practice (*al-'adm*): whoever invokes established practice shall have his claim stand. Contradictory claims shall bear the burden of proof. Established practice is that the status quo shall remain until proven otherwise, and established practice regarding things is passive consent until proof is established that they are prohibited..."

If we consult the constitution, we find that Article 3 stipulates: "Islamic *sharia* shall be the primary source of legislation."

Article 4 of the constitution stipulates that "authority shall rest in the people."

We also find that Article 26 stipulates that: "Every citizen shall be entitled to participate in political, economic, social, and cultural life. The state shall guarantee freedom of thought and freedom to express his opinion through speech, writing, and representation within the limits of the law..."

Article 39 stipulates: "So long as it does not contravene the constitution, citizens throughout the republic shall have the right to form political, professional, and trade union organizations, as well as educational, cultural, and social organizations and national federations that serve the goals of the constitution. The state shall guarantee this right...and all means necessary shall be used to enable citizens to exercise said right. All freedoms shall be guaranteed to political, trade union, cultural, educational, and social institutions and organizations."

While the Elections Law does not contain an explicit statement of prohibition or lack of permission for domestic or international monitoring of elections, it also does not contain an explicit statement allowing it. Therefore, in such cases, established practice is followed, which is passive consent and non-prohibition, as your committee decided on February 14, 1993. Your committee was also in agreement when it stated in its decision that it would formulate guidelines for monitoring. This is necessary for the general welfare of the country in order to prevent conflict and clashes, thereby enabling matters to proceed in a manner serving the goals and aims of the public as represented by complete freedom, impartiality, and neutrality in the parliamentary elections of April 27, 1993. This will confirm statements made at home and abroad by all the highest leaders of the country to the effect that they are pursuing democratic rule and the peaceful exchange of authority. The NCFE has prepared schedules and manual for volunteer monitors explaining that the NCFE and its volunteers are bound by the Elections Law, the election guide prepared by the Supreme Election Committee, and the instructions of the latter and that the work of the committee is monitoring, not intervention in any activities of the Supreme Election Committee or of its supervisory committees or subcommittees. We have attached a copy of the above and have stressed the preceding through training courses for volunteers conducted by the NCFE in the Capital, Aden, Ta'izz, al-Hudaydah, Dhamar and Hajjah governorates in cooperation with the National Democratic Institute and several international monitors from Bulgaria, Romania, Bangladesh, and Kenya.

Brother Chairman, Vice Chairman, and members of the Supreme Election Committee:

We have written to you at this particular stage because we have contacted Chairman of the Legal Committee Prof. Abd-al-Fattah al-Basir several times to obtain the legal guidelines for our work and to coordinate the presence of monitors at polling places in implementation of your venerable committee's aforementioned decision. We have done so because we were surprised by a statement issued by your venerable committee on [blank] referring to welcoming international election monitors and stating that the Elections Law stipulates in two articles (Nos. 61 and 67) sufficient monitoring for candidates, in addition to the other guarantee represented by membership of your committee and its subcommittees.

Although this statement does not state explicitly that your venerable committee reversed its aforementioned decision, the implication for some in its latest statement was that it had reversed its previous decision without informing us. This prompted us to write to you explaining all the preceding facts about the NCFE and its work as of this date.

We also call your attention to the fact that using the spirit of Articles 61 and 67 of the Elections Law as a basis is not sufficient, nor are the circumstances, to rule that domestic monitoring of elections is not permissible. Furthermore, to say that there is sufficient domestic monitoring and to allow only international monitoring is erroneous, as we will show:

**Fact one:**

The Law established a similar right for the candidate or his representative to enter or to be present on election day for the personal protection and interest of the candidate. The presence of a domestic monitor is to protect a public right of concern to voters and society. In his neutral capacity, the monitor will not be present to protect a private interest, as the candidate will, but to monitor the election.

In short he will be present to eliminate the causes of corruption, prevent doubts, and represent society through the nature of the committee, since there are thousands of volunteers from different parts of the country.

**Fact two:**

The candidate, or his representative, has the right to be present on election day in order to give him the necessary assurance that the result was based on vote sorting procedures carried out in his presence or in the presence of his representative. The presence of a domestic monitor will be to provide neutral assurance that all election procedures, up to time the results are known, were carried out properly, in an orderly fashion, and totally in accordance with the Elections Law. In this way, public assurance will be given to the voters and to society.

**Fact three:**

The two preceding facts show that candidates do not constitute domestic election monitors because they or their representatives are present in the election room for reasons different from those of monitors and because their tasks and activities differ.

**Fact four:**

The decision of the Supreme Election Committee in its most recent statement confirms its decision on the principle of the existence of domestic election monitoring. Legally a principle is indivisible, and as long as the door is open for international monitoring, which is an approved political effort, domestic monitoring is legitimized because elections affect the welfare of Yemeni society, which is concerned with the results, and because "those who are nearest should have priority."

**Fact five:**

Because we have no experience or practice in election monitoring, the NCFE has cooperated with the National Democratic Institute and certain international monitors to benefit from international expertise in this field. This has become known to the rest of the world as the existence of domestic monitoring. Restricting the choice to international monitoring without domestic monitoring, as some see it, will portray the country and the entire election in a fashion totally incompatible with the goals of your venerable committee. It will have the opposite effect, creating doubt about the motive for rejecting domestic monitoring, which is a basis and foundation of international monitoring. This is true unless the committee considers its advice and decisions binding, for the rest of the world to approve, in which case there would be no need for domestic or international monitoring.

**Fact six:**

Your venerable committee also hopes to win the trust of the rest of the world for sound election practices and procedures by welcoming the presence of international monitors to ensure the impartiality and soundness of the elections. It must first confirm this to voters inside the country so that they will accept the election and be assured that their votes will go to their chosen candidates.

Party workers do not form a large percentage of voters. We cannot be certain that the political parties and organizations, which are the cohesive element in the birth of the Republic of Yemen and the democratic transformation, represent all the wishes of the people. Their number of organized members is smaller than that group of society that is not part of the party framework. The presence of domestic monitors cannot be invalidated by these weak claims.

**Conclusion**

You will have observed that the goals of your venerable committee are the same as those of the NCFE: free, impartial elections that will reassure society at home and abroad. For this reason, cooperation between the NCFE and your committee has been envisioned and is desired because we have a single goal.

For these reasons, the NCFE encourages the Supreme Election Committee to facilitate its task and enable it to achieve the country's greatest aspirations: confidence, stability, and the establishment of sound democratic traditions, which will make the Supreme Election Committee a democratic institution in its own right in the view of the people and of international organizations.

We hope for a positive response and completion of domestic monitoring procedures.

*Appendix XIII*

# Statement by NCFE Asking for Public Support in Dispute with SEC Regarding Written Permission to Monitor Elections

16 March 1993

### Statement by Mr. Ahmed Othman

### NCFE's Vice Chairman for External Affairs

In late January 1993, the National Committee for Free Elections (NCFE) has been formed in the Republic of Yemen (ROY). Its main urgent action was to recruit and train Yemeni literate and non-partisans or candidates, who will observe elections' operations and make sure that any elections take place in the country be free, fair and agree with international standards.

The NCFE is an independent organization of Yemeni citizens who are pledged to monitor the elections in a non-partisan and honest way. It is, therefore, supported by all major Yemeni parties as well as by international friends and observers.

The Executive board of the NCFE is as follows:

- Mr. Mustafa Ahmed Muhammad Noman, President (01-725099, 270636, 77318);
- Mr. Ahmed Muhammad 'Ali Othman, Vice President for External Affairs (01-216220);
- Dr. Ahmed Noman Kassim Almadhagi, Executive Director (01-238733);
- Ibtisam Muhammad Alhamdi, Director of Finance (01-2206483);
- Ahmed Alsoofi, Director of Information/spokesman (01-204506);
- Dr. Salim Altamimi;
- Mr. Hafidh 'Abd Allah Fadhil, Director of Lawyers Group (01-273927).

To attain legal status, the NCFE has to be established as a sub-committee of the non-governmental organization, the Yemeni

Organization for the Defence of Rights and Freedoms (YODRF). Under international pressure, including that of the US National Democratic Institute for International Affairs' support, the Supreme Election Commission (SEC) in the ROY has on 14 February 1993 approved the role of the NCFE and publicly pledged to facilitate its role.

At the special meeting that was held at 10 a.m. of 21 February between the SEC vice-chairman, Muhammad Sai'd Abd 'Allah and Mr. Thomas Melia, Program Director of the NDI, and was attended by Dr. Ahmed Noman Almadhagi, the executive director of the NCFE, the NDI's national and international delegates and volunteers who are interested in observing the elections were welcomed. Two hours later, at the SEC's meeting with foreign diplomats and attended by the NDI's representative and NCFE's executive director, the SEC vice-chairman confirmed in a reply to a question by the Kuwaiti Chargé, that the Yemeni elections experiment does not belong to the Yemeni people alone, but it does also belong to the international community. "It is a human and universal experiment in Yemen. We welcome international observation of our elections. We have already agreed to facilitate the NCFE and the NDI's missions", Mr. Muhammad Sai'd 'Abd Allah confirmed.

What was officially pledged, however, was not the real policy of the SEC. Its legal department holdup arrangements, including the written permission of NCFE's operations. Consequently, access to public means of communication was denied and NCFE's efforts to recruit volunteers were obstructed by the SEC's unclear policy. It appeared that a faction of the SEC was wasting the NCFE's time and throwing thorns in its way: several so-called organizations were asked to apply to the SEC for the same purpose and several SEC leading officials were undermining the NCFE's mission.

Between 14 February and 15 March 1993, the NCFE continued its contacts with the SEC in order to obtain written recognition of its status by the SEC in order to be able to function better by using, for example, the public media in its endeavour to recruit and educate its volunteers who will be monitoring the supposedly first free and fair election in the history of ROY; it also held five meetings with representatives of Yemeni parties, which the NCFE has asked to form the advisory board of the NCFE. On the 15th March meeting, the NCFE was promised by all parties including the General Peoples

Congress (PGC), the religious al-Tajamu' al-Yamani al-Islah and the Yemeni Socialist Party (YSP), that, in the subsequent 16 March meeting, they would nominate representatives to the Advisory Board as well as they would nominate seven additional nonpartisan members to join the executive committee of the NCFE. Meanwhile, between 9 and 15 March, the NCFE has, with the cooperation and assistance of the NDI, held several training conferences in six major cities of the ROY. 593 partisan and nonpartisan individuals were trained by NDI's international training teams at seven conferences held in Sana'a, Aden, Taiz, Dhamar, Hudaidah, Hajah. But the SEC's stand was disappointing to the NCFE.

On the 15th of February, while the NCFE was discussing its plans to recruit and train around 8,000 independent observers and was waiting for the parties to fulfil their promises, it was surprised to hear a SEC statement to the Yemeni media that denied any national nonpartisan organization the right to observe the 27th April Parliamentary elections on the basis that the Yemeni Constitution did not permit such a role for non-partisan observers; political parties' monitoring role was secured.

Although shocked by such a statement by the SEC at a time parties had pledged their support to its independent and popular operations, the NCFE, while assuring foreign diplomatic missions that it would continue its legal role, hopes that the governmental democratic institutions throughout the world should double their support to the Yemeni peoples' cause — their right to have free and fair parliamentary elections scheduled 27th April. The NCFE also hopes that international organizations will show their moral and any sort of support to the Committee's role in the ROY.

It urges all friends of Yemen and all supporters of democratic development to provide moral support to the NCFE's task by questioning the current policies of the government of ROY. The NCFE welcomes foreign assistance, advice and campaigning in support of free and fair elections in the ROY. Support to Yemen's democratic orientation could be achieved through sending more foreign delegations to monitor Yemeni elections; through training NCFE's volunteers; through questioning the substance of Yemen's democracy; through sending journalists to the ROY; through talking to Yemeni officials about the SEC's prohibition of internal independent observation; and through advising international observation teams to contact the NCFE and coordinate their efforts with the NCFE's men and women who volunteered to end violations of civic and human rights in this country.

The NCFE is currently occupying offices of the YODRF throughout the country. For more information, international supporters of democratic development are welcome to contact NCFE's officials or coordinators in the major governorates of the ROY.

The pressing goal of the NCFE and all of its volunteers is to make the scheduled parliamentary elections on 27 April 1993 honest, free and fair elections that should be conducted peacefully and in accordance with the law and international standards. Our friends all over the world are invited to support and advise us on how to make free and fair elections in the ROY a reality.

Issued in Sana'a, Republic of Yemen

On 15 March 1993

*Appendix XIV*

# Undated Letter from NCFE to SEC Stating NCFE Goals and Seeking Approval and Cooperation

The Honorable Mr. Kadi 'Abdul-Karim al-'Arashi
Member of Presidential Council; Chairman of SEC

Peace Be Upon You!

With reference to our letter dated February 6, which was delivered to you by Mr. Abd 'Allah al-Hakimi member of SEC, and was directed by yourself to the legal sub-committee [on February 14] to prepare the SEC response to the NCFE, I here emphasize the following:

1. The objective behind the formation of the NCFE is to facilitate the SEC work, through the former's neutral and objective presence at the poll's centers; 2. One of the NCFE objectives is to promote popular participation in elections. This should lead to further popular understanding of the democratic process, and thus would lead to wide popular acceptance of the results of elections; 3. The NCFE is hoping to cooperate with the NCFE. It would participate in promoting awareness of the role of the SEC as well as facilitating it; 4. The training of our nonpartisan volunteers leads to thorough understanding of Elections Law and of related documents prepared by the SEC. We hope that you don't consider such an activity a sort of interference in your work — our training could be categorized in this context as a general information effort.

We were pleased to know that your committee has approved our role on February 14, and that you have instructed the legal sub-committee to issue the necessary regulations to facilitate this role.

We were surprised after a long interval that your committee has approved international observation of elections, but denied local popular NCFE such a role. What overwhelmed us more is the way Election Law was interpreted to deny us the right to monitor elections.

Once again, I want to assure you that we do want to cooperate with you, and that we will respect the regulations you set for us in this regard.

Finally, we want to express our appreciation of all the SEC patriotic achievements, which were accomplished under your supervision.

Regards and thanks,

Mustafa A.M. Noman
Chairman

*Appendix XV*

# Letter from Rep. Lee Hamilton
# to President Saleh

March 30, 1993

His Excellency Ali Abdullah Salih
President
Republic of Yemen
Sana'a, Yemen

Dear Mr. President,

I write to express the hope that the upcoming elections on April 27th will be both free and fair and will serve as an important model and symbol of leadership for the Middle East and Persian Gulf. You can take a considerable measure of pride in what you have achieved to now.

Many of us in Washington have been following with great interest the development of the political situation in Yemen, and we have been heartened by much of what we have heard. Your invitation to the international community to send experts and observers to prepare for and observe the April elections is widely welcomed.

Accordingly, I was pleased to learn that, following a meeting in Washington with Foreign Minister Abdal-Karim al-Iryani, the National Democratic Institute for International Affairs sent an international team to assess the electoral environment and to explore ways in which assistance could be provided in support of democratization. As you know, the Institute has organized highly-regarded observer missions to elections on every continent. I have been advised that NDI has entered into an agreement with Yemen's National Committee for Free Elections to train local volunteers to observe the April elections. This agreement is an important step toward free and fair elections.

Recently, I have been apprised by NDI that there appears to be an effort underway by some to try to undermine the work of the National Committee for Free Elections. I am sure you will agree that it would be unfortunate if Yemen's many accomplishments in recent months were to be obscured by the shortsighted factions of a few overzealous officials or party workers. I am writing therefore, to suggest that the Supreme Election Committee be urged to consider carefully how the work of the National Committee for Free Elections can be constructive in the elections process and how important it is for the National Committee to be independent and impartial so that its important role in the election process is not undermined.

I appreciate your consideration of this important concern which has been stated to me and I wish you a successful and democratic election in late April.

With best regards,

Sincerely,

Lee H. Hamilton
Chairman

LHH/MVD:kpw

*Appendix XVI*

# Letter from Sen. Daniel Patrick Moynihan, et. al., to President Saleh

April 2, 1993

His Excellency Lt. Gen. Ali Abdullah Saleh
Chairman of the Presidency Council
Zubiary Street
Sana'a, Yemen

Dear President Saleh:

We are writing to bring to your attention disturbing reports that we have received concerning recent developments in Yemen regarding the preparations for multiparty elections on April 27.

As you know, international observers have been following with great interest the development of the political situation in Yemen and have been encouraged by the steps your society is taking toward democracy. Your invitation to the international community to send observers to the April elections was widely welcomed.

It is our understanding that, following a meeting in Washington with Foreign Minister Abdul Karia al-Eryani, the National Democratic Institute (NDI) sent an international team to explore ways to assist the process of democratization in Yemen. As you may know, NDI is a highly respected non-governmental organization engaged in democratic political development work on every continent. We understand that NDI agreed to cooperate with Yemen's National Committee for Free Elections to train local volunteers to observe the April elections.

We believe that the work of the National Committee for Free Elections — as an independent, non-governmental organization — is vitally important to securing the credibility of the fairness of your upcoming elections. The international community — and the United States Congress in particular — will want to know that its activities were not restricted or hindered.

It is therefore disturbing to receive reports that there appears to be a concerted effort underway in some quarters to undermine the work of the National Committee and to discredit and obstruct its activities. Inevitably, the Government of Yemen will be held responsible — and the international credibility of the upcoming elections will suffer badly — if certain overzealous officials or party functionaries interfere with the ability of the National Committee to provide an independent assessment of the fairness of the elections.

We hope that you will promptly take every appropriate step to ensure that the National Committee for Free Elections is permitted to pursue its activities without hindrance.

Sincerely,

Sen. Daniel Patrick Moynihan
Chairman, Subcommittee on
 Near Eastern and South
 Asian Affairs, Committee
 on Foreign Relations

Sen. Hank Brown
Ranking Member, Subcommittee
 on Near Eastern and South
 Asian Affairs, Committee on
 Foreign Relations

Sen. Claiborne Pell
Chairman, Committee on
 Foreign Relations

Sen. Jim Jeffords

Sen. Edward Kennedy

*Appendix XVII*

# Letter from Foreign Minister Al-Eryani to Rep. Lee Hamilton

April 6, 1993

The Honorable Congressman Lee H. Hamilton
Chairman, Committee on Europe and Middle East
United States House of Representatives
2187 Rayburn House Office Building
Washington, D.C.  20515-1409

Dear Congressman Hamilton:

On behalf of the Chairman of the Presidential Council, Ali Abdullah Saleh, I want to thank you for your recent letter expressing encouragement for the democratic process in the Republic of Yemen and concern for activities of the National Committee for Free Elections.  We in Yemen are pleased to know that the international community is watching our elections with interest.

First let me say that we appreciate very much the efforts of the National Democratic Institute, the International Republican Institute, the International Foundation for Electoral Systems, and the numerous European election organizations that have visited Yemen and offered advice and assistance in connection with our upcoming parliamentary election, we recognize that the expertise that these organizations can provide will be very beneficial to us as we proceed through this election and seek to institutionalize democracy for the future.

Regarding your inquiry into the activities of the National Committee for Free Elections, I would like to assure you that this organization and the other domestic organizations that have been formed with the same objective are absolutely free and encouraged to train local persons to act as election observers and we hope that the National Democratic Institute will continue to work with them in this regard.  However, our election law requires that election monitors be appointed by candidates, and does not permit self-appointment. Therefore, the only restriction on the activities of the National Committee for Free Elections and the other domestic organizations working on election monitoring is that the individual monitor be appointed by a candidate for office. We understand from various election groups that are expert in parliamentary elections that this is consistent with practices in numerous countries like ours in the early stages of democratic development.

The Supreme Election Committee has received numerous requests for a waiver of our election law to permit domestic election organizations to enter the polling place in a capacity other than as a candidate's representative. However, the committee, which includes eleven separate party representatives and two independent members, has decided against granting such waivers because the Committee believes that the outcome of such an experiment would most likely be the creation of controversy and confusion. With over forty parties participating in our elections, the Supreme Election Committee felt that adequate monitoring capability would be provided by the candidates' representatives. The Supreme Election Committee has assure me that it strongly supports the National Democratic Institute's training efforts, and believes that the best and most constructive approach to monitoring efforts by the National Committee for Free Elections and other similar groups is to reach out to the individual candidates and parties and provide training and resources, including offering their own pool of qualified representatives, so that the greatest number of pollwatchers can be reached and trained, and the greatest possible number of candidates represented.

I would like to emphasize our appreciation for the efforts of the National Democratic Institute and all the other election groups involved. It is the sincere desire of the people of the Republic of Yemen that these groups remain involved in the democratic process have not only through the elections, but after them as well to help us to consolidate our democratic process and develop the democratic institutions so crucial to all democratic societies. I can assure you that every effort will be made to accommodate the requests and concerns of all of the international groups working here including the provision of unrestricted access to polling places and complete freedom to meet privately with any Yemeni citizen, party or group they choose.

Finally, I would like to invite you and all of the members of the Foreign Affairs Committee, along with your staff, to attend our elections on April 27 to observe first hand the way in which the election is held.  I firmly believe that there is no substitute for first hand knowledge and very much hope to have the opportunity to welcome you personally in Yemen for this historic election.

Thank you again for expressing interest in our upcoming election.

Sincerely,

Abdul Karim al-Eryani

Minister of Foreign Affairs
Republic of Yemen

*Appendix XVIII*

# YCFDE Press Statement Regarding Perceived Impartiality of an International Organization

YEMEN COMMITTEE FOR FREE &
DEMOCRATIC ELECTIONS

## Press Release

For more information contact Abdulkareem Al-Magadeh

### An International Organization Chooses Not to Observe Impartiality

Sana'a,  24 April 1993

The Yemen Committee for Free and Democratic Elections while watching the preparation for the country's first legislative elections, is pleased to express admiration for the work done by the Supreme Election Committee (SEC) to ensure free and fair elections.

For our part as a committee with an objective to support the democratic process in the country, we were hoping to take part side by side with international observers in observing the elections away from the influence of political parties.  At the same time, we express our dismay over an international organization decision to side with one committee by giving it political and financial support and ruled out any dealings with other committees present in the field today, even though: the committee they have chosen to support has well-known affiliation with some political parties.

The YCDFE, an independent Committee established by concerned citizens to support the democratic process in the country, is surprised by the attitude adopted by both the Yemen Committee and the foreign organization that supports it.  If by such attitude, we are to think that someone has given mandate to monopolize local observation, we say NO.  You are not alone and we are all in the same boat given that no decision has been taken on this matter by the SEC.

If indeed someone cares for the democratic process and the impartiality of the elections process Yemen, we believe, we should be working together with him.

*Appendix XIX*

# NDI Memorandum in Response to YCFDE Statement Regarding Perceived Impartiality

Memorandum to International Election Observers in Yemen

From:     Thomas O. Melia
          Program Director
          National Democratic Institute

Date:     April 25, 1993

Subject:  "Committee for Free and Democratic Elections"
          or "Imitation is the Sincerest Form of Flattery"

A press release from the 'Yemen Committee for Free and Democratic Elections' dated April 24 (attached) has just been brought to my attention. It is headlined: "An International Organization Chooses not to Observe Impartiality."

Although the text of the statement is strangely circumlocutious — referring ominously and vaguely to unspecified but "well-known political affiliations" of unnamed international and Yemeni organizations — officers of the YCFDE have today informed us that their intention was to refer to the work of the National Democratic Institute to support the National Committee for Free Elections (NCFE). Accordingly, it may be of interest to some observers to have a fuller record of the efforts made by NDI to support Yemeni domestic election observers.

An account of our work with the NCFE is contained in an April 21 report by NDI entitled "Promoting Popular Participation in Yemen's Elections." (Additional copies are available from me in Room 604 of the Taj Sheba Hotel.) Regarding our contact and cooperation with the YCFDE, the brief chronology below may be useful.

It is the policy of the National Democratic Institute to offer its information-sharing and training programs to interested democrats on an inclusive, nonpartisan basis. NDI has a well-established international reputation for nonpartisanship in its work in support of democratic election processes. Because the origins of the YCFDE lie so unambiguously in an effort by certain members of the People's General Congress to undermine the operation of the independent National Committee for Free Elections, we have naturally been somewhat circumspect in our dealings with it. At the same time, in the interest of wider dissemination of information about international practices in democratic institution-building (and in the hope that something positive might emerge from the YCFDE), NDI staff in Yemen have repeatedly extended practical assistance to the YCFDE.

### March 10 to 16

An international team of trainers travels with NCFE staff to several locations around Yemen and assists in the conduct of training and orientation sessions at which approximately 500 Yemenis are present. Branches of the NCFE are established in most governorates.

### March 16, 17 and 18

On the margins of several all-parties meetings convened by the NCFE in the continuing effort to address PGC and al-Islah concerns about the operation of the NCFE, NDI representatives participated in numerous extended and private conversations with PGC representatives to these meetings. The principal discussion during these days was about the PGC proposal to add seven persons it would designate to the existing seven person executive committee of the NCFE — to "ensure that the NCFE would remain nonpartisan and independent." NDI was informed that, if PGC demands to take control of the NCFE were not met, "we will create *our own* group of local monitors — with more money, more access, more media coverage."

### [NDI staff departs March 19]

### March 30

NDI staff person Melissa Estok arrives at Sana'a airport at the start of a weeklong pre-election survey mission. She is unexpectedly met at the airport by two men who inform her that they were sent by Muhammed al-Tayeb of the PGC to talk with her. Their names: Abdul Rahman Al-Moaseb and Hamoud al-Dafiry. They inform Ms. Estok that they have been asked by Mr. al-Tayeb on behalf of the

PGC to organize domestic observers for the elections, to be called the Committee for Free and Democratic Elections. They ask for preliminary information about the purpose and tasks of domestic observers.

### March 31

Ms. Estok spends two hours with the two men and provides them with copies of various NDI publications relating to election monitoring and informs them our of ongoing work with the NCFE, and encourages them top contact the NCFE to see about collaboration.

They request copies of training manuals that they believe NDI has provided to the NCFE. They are informed that the NCFE developed its own training materials and operational guidelines, based on information and advice it received from NDI (including principally the same written materials that were supplied to Mr. Al-Moaseb and Dr. al-Dafiry) and from the international team that had been present in Yemen in mid-March.

### April 7

A fax addressed to Estok arrives at the hotel requesting NDI assistance. The fax erroneously notes that an NDI team of international trainers is to arrive in Yemen April 10. [This may be based on a preliminary timeline of NDI activities prepared in early February that was apparently made available to the YCFDE by Yemeni government officials.]

### April 8

Estok speaks by phone with Abdul Karim al-Magalah of the YCFDE, reiterating NDI's interest in cooperation, encouraging the YCFDE to meet with the NCFE, and noting that she is engaged for a couple more days with the pre-election delegation of six persons that is still in Yemen conducting interviews.

### April 10

A second fax letter arrives from the YCFDE reiterating a general request for assistance.

### April 12

Estok and Bob Norris (recently arrived from NDI in Washington) meet with YCFDE leaders, who request funding from

NDI and copies of the manuals they erroneously think NDI prepared for the NCFE. Their comments indicated that they believe that NDI has provided $600,000 to the NCFE.

[Again, this seems to be based on a misreading of official documents. The U.S. Agency for International Development has expended approximately $600,000 in various programs to assist the electoral process in Yemen. A portion of that, approximately $50,000, was earmarked for the pre-election survey conducted by NDI. None of it was for the NCFE. From other funding, NDI has entered a cooperative agreement with NCFE to provide approximately $40,000 to finance the printing and travel and telephone expenses of the NCFE during a three-month period. To date, $10,000 has actually been provided to the NCFE.]

Norris and Estok reiterate the standing offer to appear personally at any training sessions that YCFDE organizes (as they have done with NCFE) to explain the work of domestic monitors and to provide advice and information.

The meeting ends with threats that "NDI will have its fingers burned" if it declines to provide funding and printed materials to the YCFDE.

### April 14

A meeting takes place between NCFE Vice Chair Ahmed al-Othman and YCFDE Chairman Abdul-Wahab Rawih to explore possible cooperation. It is agreed that a fuller meeting of the two committees will take place on April 16.

### April 16

Dr. Rawih cancels the expected meeting, citing the need to prepare for a training program for his local monitors on the 17th and 18th. [Apparently the training program does not take place.]

### April 18

NDI staffers Norris and Estok meet with several persons from the YCFDE. YCFDE presents familiar requests for printed materials and funding. Norris and Estok reiterate offer to attend any further meetings with YCFDE volunteers.

### April 19

Overnight a note has been slipped under Estok's hotel room door inviting her to appear at a YCFDE volunteer training session that has been scheduled for the morning of the 19th. Estok is en route at that moment to a plane to Mukalla for previously scheduled training session of volunteers of the NCFE. By the time Norris found the message and called the YCFDE later in the day, he was told it was too late to attend. [This is the meeting at which 20 YCFDE volunteers were trained.]

### April 22

Following a late night arrival from Aden, Estok the next morning finds a note under her hotel door inviting her to a training session scheduled by the YCFDE. Estok and Norris try to call during the day to YCFDE to arrange earlier notice of these events, but are not successful in reaching YCFDE in time to attend the April 22 meeting.

### April 23

Melia returns to Yemen and attends a *qat* session at the home of PGC official Hamdanni. There he sees printed copies of 'election monitoring forms' printed [in English] by the YCFDE. They are very similar to first drafts prepared by the NCFE a couple of weeks earlier, and provided by Mustapha Noman to officials of the PGC. While the NCFE has subsequently refined their documents before printing and distribution, the YCFDE has reprinted the earlier versions with slight modifications.

### April 24

The NCFE prepares the first of an envisioned daily bulletin for international observers notifying them of activities of the NCFE. It is distributed by 6 a.m. to journalists and observers. By 7 p.m. the YCFDE has duplicated and distributed its version of this document, too.

*Appendix XX*

# YCFDE Memorandum in Response to NDI Memorandum

| | |
|---|---|
| Date | 26-4-1993 |
| Reference | NDI-4-93 |

YEMEN COMMITTEE FOR FREE &
DEMOCRATIC ELECTIONS

A reply to a memorandum to International observers in Yemen issued by Mr. Thomas O. Melia, Program Director, National Democratic Institute.

Mr. Thomas O. Melia
National Democratic Institute
Sheba Hotel Sana'a Rm 604

Date April 26, 1993

Subject "Your Memo of 25/4/1993 to International Elections Observers in Yemen"

Dear Mr O'Melia

We were very happy to receive a phone call from you on the 24th of April to arrange a meeting with us for future cooperation and we said to ourselves, Finally, NDI has come to recognize that the democratic process in Yemen means plurality of ideas and organizations working to attain this objective; but to our dismay, we found out the contrary — a continuation of a series of rejections based on misconceptions which the memo brought to light and we thank God for that.

When two of our officers, Dr. Hamoud Al-Dafiry and Abdulkareem Al-Magaleh met with you at the Taj Sheba Hotel Lobby at 12.00 O'clock noon on the 25th of April 1993, they were confronted with a question that the press release issued by our committee was meant against the NDI or not. Although they did not specifically mention NDI in the face of your insistence that NDI should be named, you went ahead and handed them over the Memo which has been prepared earlier and was ready for distribution and which had already stated that the officers told you that your Institute is the subject of the press release. When in fact, this never happened. This goes to prove the Misconception held by your staff and apparently by you about our Committee from the start. We were always looking for answers to the continuous unconcealed effort to defray us from going a head with our effort forge some kind of relationship with your organization and other international observers for the sake of learning from them and exchanging ideas on the democratic process and on the election observation procedures and your memo gave us the answers.

Your statement made under the name our Committee "Imitation is the sincerest form of flattery" goes to prove that the non-impartiality mentioned in our press release is in fact true and that you are biased and wanted to deal with one committee and didn't want to bother yourself with helping others. You may be right in adopting this attitude and you are free to do so; but this could have been told to us from the start instead of responses which gave us eerie feelings that we were unwelcomed before we had the chance to introduce ourselves.

As for the reputation of NDI as a nonpartisanship organization, we recognize this fact and the reason why we started contacting you from the start. But as mentioned above, your staff continued "scoff offs" led us to believe that your dealings didn't reflect non-partisanship because you only preferred to deal with one committee. In this case, you may have been misled.

Your allegation that the origin of our committee lies unambiguously in an effort by certain members of the Peoples General Congress to undermine the operation of NCFE, you alone have made this conclusion and the examples you cited in your memo make a very interesting case of analogies and appear to be convincing. But the fact is, our committee has nothing to do with the PGC or for that matter any other political party and we have been firm believers of non-partisanship given that all our members are no affiliated with any political organization or party in the country. In the same paragraph, you mentioned that NDI staff have repeatedly extended practical assistance to the YCFDE. We can not help but say that such a statement do not reflect the intention and we would like to say that (NO) such assistance, practical or otherwise has been extended by any of NDI staff to our committee. We mentioned above, that whenever we contact any of your staff, we are met with what amounts to a total rejection of any dealings with us for reasons we only realized through your memo. We can only say that you have been misled and we hope that this will serve to encourage you to correct the erroneous notions your staff have been holding about our committee.

As for the agreement that a fuller meeting between our committee and the NCFE which was scheduled for the 16th of April was canceled. This only happened after Dr. Rawih approached the officials of NCFE and was confronted with unacceptable conditions for our cooperation mainly a signed certificate from all political parties working in the field that they are comfortable with us and a set of other conditions.

The notes slipped under the door, we assure you, aren't the work of our committee but the work of the hotel staff who write messages for all the guests in the hotel who are out. The reason why we resorted to leaving messages was for the sole reason that your staff were simply not in the hotel and as an inexperienced committee as we are, the schedules of your staffers are not known to us to make sure that we don't inform you at the right time. As you know and as we have always been repeating we are a new organization, and we need all the help we can get from experienced organizations like yours, but surely this attitude did not help us and we were left to whatever little experience and the good faith we have on our objectives and the mandate we set for our committee.

Your mention of a meeting on the 18th of April that took place between YCFDE officers and NDI staffers Bob Norris and Estok, such a meeting never took place but there was a telephone conversation between Mr. Norris and Abdulkareem Al-Magaleh on the 19th of April about the training session that day. Mr. Norris was requested to give us any printed material NDI may have put out to help us with our effort, but we were met with the familiar response that the material has been given to the NCFE and he will see if he can get us a copy and that never materialized too.

Our request for technical assistance from your side stems from our believe that NDI is a reputable organization with respected experience in the field and we wanted to benefit from such experience not knowing that you have chosen not to deal with us from the start due to misconceptions held about our committee.

Other accounts in your memo, go to prove that you think we are a real imitation of the NCFE and this, consequently, proves, that you hold certain bias in favour of the latter and your trying to defend them and protect their activities at any cost. A clear example, was your mention of the NCFE envisioned daily bulletin, which we didn't know that it was meant to be as such. But we would like to assure you that we started to issue press releases way before this occurrence the first of which was announcement of our training sessions. We haven't duplicated nor distributed any versions of this document except for our press releases which were meant to give background information to members of the press on activities of our committee which we have worked so hard to organize and we strive to make known.

Your account of our fax addressed to Ms. Estok on April the 7th was intentionally toned to reflect your misconception about the real intentions of our committee. We sincerely required such assistance to help us with our training effort. The misreading of your schedule was due to the fact that we are not in constant contacts with your organization to know that you have revised the schedule. The information we got about your schedule we obtained from one of our members and we think there is nothing wrong with that, unless you wanted your cooperation with the NCFE to remain secret. In this case, we apologize for infringing upon such secrecy and hope it benefits democracy in Yemen.

And your account of Ms. Estok's conversation on April 8th with Abdulkareem Al-Magaleh and your mentioned that Ms. Estok "reiterating NDI's interest in cooperation, encouraging the YCFDE to meet with the NCFE." There were no mention of such a thing during the conversation and the only thing she said was that she was engaged in the preparation of a report that she has to write and would call back to arrange for a meeting which she never did. This was another incident which reflected the familiar attitude of NDI staffers.

The repetitive mention for our requests for assistance in your memo give the impression that we are interested only in assistance, money and otherwise. We assure you again that our requests, which never received a satisfactory response, written or otherwise and were totally ignored, stems from the advice of other international organizations including IFES that you are the only organization which conducts training for observers (Copy of IFES fax message to this fact is enclosed). As for our mention of the funds available for the purpose your mission in Yemen it was not meant to be taken in such a light but simply a mention of information we have (and could be wrong) and how you go about spending it this is a matter which doesn't concern us.

In the meeting of the 12th of April with NDI staffers, we hoped to be sincere in our dealings and we tried to pin point some of the facts we know and were never meant as threats . Reference was made to your meetings on the 16, 17 and 18 of March with Mr. Mohamed Al-Tayeb, this is a matter of no concern to us, but it was included in the memo to drive at the point that we are connected to him — an effort to push further the drive by NCFE and NDI to discredit our committee. This is simply a gross miscalculation of events and the correlation between experiences of your staffers and our committee has been false. We have contacted Mr. Al-Tayeb about this and has informed us he will make a written response to your allegations.

And about our officers meeting your staffer, Ms. Estok at the airport, We have enquired about this and found out that Dr Hamoud Al-Dafiry never met her at the airport but at the hotel and went together to the airport to meet two ladies from Turkey. Mr Al-Dafiry has denied that he said he was sent by Mohamed Al-Tayeb but gave her an indication that our committee was being formed-we think this is a normal thing to do given the fact that we are seeking the cooperation of international organizations with similar objectives.

Again, we think that the memo carries wrong conclusions and statements about our committee at a time when the objective should have been how to promote organizations like ours for the sake of sound democratic practices and institutional building.

We intended to go a head with the idea of establishing an Institute for domestic observation and democratic studies to promote the idea of institutionalizing the democratic process in Yemen to avoid a retreat to the practices of the past which hindered the country's development. Our main objective is to effect the peaceful transformation into a real democratic society and we will build on the idea that brought us into being. This election, although important, is the first election and there will be many other elections which we hope we will make real contributions to.

In concluding, we thank the IRI observers and the other observation delegations for observing non-partisanship for the sake of an objective assessment of the situation. We wish all success to your organization and hope you'll realize the truth now or latter and confirm our willingness to cooperate with you in the future if all your misconceptions have been cleared. We would also like to remind you that impartiality is the essence of democracy and one can attain it by remaining objective to information and data.

With best regards

Dr Abdul-Wahab Rawih
Chairman

*Appendix XXI*

# NCFE Election-Day
# Voter Questionnaire

Ballot center:

Constituency:

District:

Governorate:

1.  Why did you vote for this person?
    Tribesman/Party/Social Status/Scientific Status/
    Election Programme

2.  Did you fill the voting card:   alone   someone helped

3.  Neutral local observers:   necessary   not necessary

4.  Have you heard about the formation of NCFE?   yes   no

5.  Have you heard of other such committees to observe the elections?   yes   no

6.  Were there any problems during the election process?   yes   no

7.  Did any of the candidates pressure the voters to vote for him?
    yes   no

8.  Have you noticed any mistakes during your voting process?
    yes   no

9.  If yes, specify:

Any other comments:

*Appendix XXII*

# NCFE News Bulletins

NCFE NEWS BULLETIN

April 25, 1993

- The National Committee for Free Elections (NCFE) will hold a press briefing today, Sunday, 25 April, 1993 at 12:30 p.m. in the Abu Nawas room at the Taj Sheba Hotel. Food and refreshments will be served. This meeting is open to all journalists.

- Yesterday's training session for volunteer election observers was a great success; 120 volunteers attended from the Governorates of Sana'a, Haja, Marib, Al-Jowf and the Sana'a Capital Trust. The training session was covered by French Television.

- Yesterday, members of the NCFE executive committee met with international observers and briefed them about our efforts over the last three months. NCFE has invited all international observers to meet with our regional volunteers when they are deployed throughout Yemen.

- As of 9 a.m. yesterday, over 4,100 Yemenis have volunteered to join the NCFE domestic observation project. More volunteers are enlisting everyday. Volunteers have agreed to be stationed at polling sites throughout election day, beginning at 7 a.m. and continuing their vigilance until all counting is completed and results are announced. Volunteers will be in continuous communication with their NCFE Governorate coordinators. Information will be transmitted to Sana'a throughout the day by telephone. Our goal is that all written information collected by volunteers will be delivered to Sana'a the following day.

- Dr. Wafa Ahmen Al-Hamzi, the NCFE Aden coordinator, has scheduled a meeting for all NCFE constituency coordinators in the governorate of Aden. The meeting will be held today at 10 a.m. at the Ministry of Commerce, Aden Branch.

For more information call the NCFE headquarters at 235810.

NCFE NEWS BULLETIN

April 26, 1993

- The national office of the NCFE reminded all volunteers and regional coordinators yesterday that peaceful election day observation activities should not interfere in any way with the conduct of the election. All volunteers have been instructed to cooperate fully with the Supreme Election Committee and to comply with all instruction from local election officials.

- Today the NCFE held a press conference at the Taj Sheba Hotel at which they explained their activities and plans for election day observation. It was attended by both Yemeni and international journalists including reporters from Germany, France, Britain and the U.S. BBC and Voice of America will report this story in their English and Arabic broadcasts. Voice of America and the BBC conducted interviews with the chairman of the committee, Mustapha Noman, and executive committee member, Ibtasam Al-Hamdi. The BBC also filmed a later meeting at NCFE headquarters where executive committee members, coordinators and other volunteers where finalizing plans for election day monitoring. In a separate BBC interview, communications director, Faris Al-Sanabani responded to questions about the domestic observation project. This story will be broadcast on BBC World Report beginning on Monday morning and will be repeated until Tuesday morning.

- NCFE committee members and volunteers attended a reception at the U.S. Ambassador's residence Sunday evening. International observers, journalists, diplomats, and other prominent figures, including SEC officials and Yemeni political party officials also attended.

- The NCFE headquarters has been overwhelmed with popular support in the last several days. Scores of additional volunteers have asked to participate in our activities. As election day approaches it is becoming more obvious that NCFE volunteers will be able to observe the vast majority of polling stations throughout Yemen on election day.

- Tomorrow is election day. NCFE is hopeful that all will go well and democracy will finally take root in Yemen. All Yemenis should be aware that unfounded rumors and unwarranted suspicion of these elections can be as harmful to the process as real disruption of the elections. NCFE will attempt to verify all reports received by volunteers, coordinators and others on election day. Only reports coming directly from the NCFE headquarters in Sana'a should be treated as official statements from the organization. These reports will have been carefully verified before official announcements are made.

### NCFE NEWS BULLETIN

April 27, 1993

- NCFE volunteers have been reminded that our election-day observation activities should not interfere in any way with the conduct of the election. We are hopeful that this first step toward a free and democratic Yemen will be a complete success.
- Our volunteers will be transmitting information throughout the day to the NCFE governorate coordinators who will be calling the headquarters in Sana'a with periodic reports. Once we have all our results and the time to analyze them we will issue a preliminary statement. A more complete statement will be issued at a press conference on Thursday morning (April 29, 1993) at 10 a.m. at the Taj Sheba Hotel.
- Journalists are invited to drop by the NCFE headquarters to observe our activities. Please call our headquarters for directions (Tel: 235810).

### NCFE NEWS BULLETIN

April 28, 1993

- The morning after — the counting continues, and so does the monitoring by NCFE volunteers. Thousands of volunteers proved their dedication to democracy yesterday by turning out to observe the process at voting centers in 14 of 18 governorates.
- A full report will be released once all the data has been collected and analyzed. Already, however, it is clear that many volunteers were allowed full access to voting centers. In other areas access was restricted, but we were able to gather valuable information anyway.

- The NCFE national communication system proved particularly effective in helping to stop the spread of unfounded rumors about problems and turmoil. Reports continue to stream into NCFE Sana'a headquarters throughout the day and into the night. By contacting our local coordinators and volunteers, NCFE has been able to dispel certain rumors, while confirming that other reported incidents did indeed occur.

- NCFE will hold a press conference in the Golden Peacock Room of the Taj Sheba Hotel at 9 a.m. on Thursday, April 29, 1993 at which we will discuss our findings to that point.

- Today, NCFE will continue, around the clock, gathering detailed reports from our national network of volunteers and coordinators. Journalists are invited to visit NCFE headquarters at the corner of al-Giadah and al-Huria streets in the building across from the Eramm Pharmacy anytime, although it is expected that comprehensive information will be available after 3 p.m. today. All are welcome to review our system of gathering information and to review the information that we have gathered to date. For more information, call NCFE headquarters at 235810.

*Appendix XXIII*

# NCFE Press Statement

NEWS RELEASE

Sana'a, Yemen, April 26, 1993 — NCFE is very concerned about rumors being spread designed to disrupt the activities of our domestic election observation project and to cause turmoil on election day. These rumors imply that NCFE volunteers will force their way into the polling centers since our accreditation to observe the elections was retracted by the SEC. We, the executive committee of the NCFE, deny and condemn these lies. We have instructed our volunteers that force should not be part of our attempts to monitor the elections. We have continuously instructed our volunteers to respect all election officials and to follow their directions and instructions. We have trained all our volunteers in this way and our volunteer instruction manual is very explicit about this. We have also used our daily bulletin to repeatedly reminded all Yemenis and international visitors of our intention to cause no disruption. These bulletins have been widely distributed in both English and Arabic. We have made daily phone calls to all coordinators to stress the need to avoid any and all confrontations at the polling centers. Our volunteers know that they should raise no objections or arguments with anyone even if they see violations of the election laws. Our goal is simply to watch, document and report observations to our headquarters in Sana'a.

We now reiterate to international observers, journalists, all authorities and the people of the Republic of Yemen that we have instructed all NCFE volunteers to cooperate with the SEC and to comply with all instructions from local election officials. Our observation activities on election day will not interfere in any way with the conduct of the elections.

*Appendix XXIV*

# NCFE Post-Election Statement

April 29, 1993

## Introduction

The National Committee for Free Elections (NCFE) is a non-partisan group of independent Yemeni citizens organized in January 1993. Our purpose has been to support the process of democratization underway in our country by mobilizing volunteers to observe the April 27 legislative elections on an objective and comprehensive basis. Because of the widespread cynicism about the intentions of the responsible authorities, it was necessary to establish a credible independent perspective on the process — to complement the important work of international observers.

Despite the retraction of formal approval of our efforts by the Supreme Election Committee (a month after it was granted on February 14) and continuous assaults on our integrity by various partisan interests, more than 4,100 men and women volunteered to be present at voting and counting centers in 14 of 18 governorates (and in 211 of the 301 constituencies).

Some of these volunteers (about 20 percent) were permitted to enter the voting stations and conduct a thorough observation throughout the day. Much of the observation was therefore conducted while volunteers were waiting in line and while voting. As many as 50 percent were eventually allowed in to the voting centers by the end of the day, while others conducted their observation from outside. Several of our volunteers were harassed by party agents or security personnel. In at least two cases that we know of, the chairmen of the voting site electoral committee called for the arrest of a peaceable NCFE volunteer, rather than simply asking him to leave.

## Illustrations of Election-Day Irregularities

Reports of election-day irregularities were many, and frequently credible. NCFE offers the following illustrative list of incidents that were investigated or confirmed by NCFE personnel.

- Illiterate voters had their votes recorded incorrectly by party agents or election officials.

In Taiz, constituency #53-D, at noon, four illiterate women found that their votes had been recorded incorrectly, against their wishes. Their complaints were disregarded.

- Voters were pressured by local election officials or party agents into voting for a particular candidate while in the voting center.

In Aden, constituency #24, a woman complained that she had been forced to vote for a candidate she did not want; In Aden constituency #20, workers were threatened with cutoff of paychecks if they did not vote for certain candidates;

- Some voters found that they were already marked on the registry as voted.

Sana'a, in constituency #11-C, six soldiers arrived and found that their voter registration numbers were listed next to different names and had been marked on the registry as having already voted. They were allowed to vote, as they had no ink on their fingers and were in possession of valid registration papers.

- Unorganized movement of ballot boxes to counting centers led to controversy and violence.

In Taiz, constituency #34-C, a dispute over how and whether candidate representatives should move with the ballot box led to the intervention of security personnel and injuries to candidate representatives.

- Many rumors of irregularities were circulating on election day. When they came to the attention of the NCFE, local volunteers were sent investigate and found many of them to be untrue.

At 13:10, a call was received from a person known to NCFE saying that there had been a shooting at voting site #12-B. Volunteers were dispatched to investigate and found the alarming story to be untrue.

At 09:45, a call came from constituency 35-C in Taiz, reporting that the chair of the women's committee had been dismissed for writing the same name for illiterate voters regardless of their stated preference. Upon investigating, NCFE found that the story was mere gossip, and that the chairwoman was still at work.

## Conclusions

1.  Numerous actions inconsistent with the spirit and the letter of the law undermined the proper conduct of the elections on April 27. Some can be attributed to SEC officials at the local level, who seemed to have received uneven or inconsistent training. More often they can be attributed to the actions of agents of political parties.

2.  Based on the information we now have, it is not clear that the outcome of any particular constituency election was altered by the election day voting or counting irregularities. Therefore, at present, our conclusion is that the announced results generally reflect the intentions of the voting population on April 27.

3.  The climate of fear and suspicion in many quarters, the minimal participation by women, and the lack of public education about democratic politics all rendered these elections less meaningful than they could have been and should have been. We hope that the next parliament and government, as well as non-governmental organizations, will address these seriously in the months ahead.

4.  After the election results are finalized, the NCFE plans to prepare a more complete report of the election process, and to offer suggestions about how the next election can be organized, in the weeks ahead.

    The NCFE thanks those who cooperated with it and all the volunteers who worked on this project to insure its success.

*Appendix XXV*

# Women's Registration Statistics

**Reproduced from the February 24 to March 2, 1993 Issue of the *Yemen Times***

**The Final Number of Registrants for the April Elections**

| Name of Governorate | Total Registrants | Total Female Registrants | Governorate's Share in Total | Governorate's Share in Female Total |
|---|---|---|---|---|
| Taiz | 423,916 | 97,586 | 15.80% | 19.60% |
| Ibb | 314,986 | 41,845 | 11.80% | 8.40% |
| Hodeidah | 310,802 | 52,429 | 11.60% | 10.50% |
| Sanaa | 289,999 | 24 | 10.80% | 5.00% |
| Sanaa City | 205,599 | 41,780 | 7.70% | 8.40% |
| Hajjah | 168,780 | 14,743 | 6.30% | 3.00% |
| Dhamar * | 160,335 | 18,005 | 6.00% | 3.60% |
| Hadhramaut ** | 154,460 | 42,289 | 5.80% | 8.50% |
| Aden | 133,653 | 47,376 | 5.00% | 9.50% |
| Lahj | 127,046 | 45,405 | 4.70% | 9.10% |
| Abyan | 83,755 | 30,829 | 3.10% | 6.20% |
| Al-Baidha | 71,098 | 11,355 | 2.60% | 2.30% |
| Saadah | 66,299 | 1,949 | 2.50% | 0.40% |
| Al-Mahweet | 60,407 | 3,007 | 2.20% | 0.60% |
| Shabwah | 51,099 | 13,890 | 1.90% | 2.80% |
| Marib | 32,204 | 5,469 | 1.20% | 1.10% |

| Name of Governorate | Total Registrants | Total Female Registrants | Governorate's Share in Total | Governorate's Share in Female Total |
|---|---|---|---|---|
| Al-Jawf | 14,838 | 310 | 0.50% | 0.06% |
| Al-Maharah | 14,555 | 4,590 | 0.50% | 0.90% |
| TOTAL | 2,684,831 | 497,662 | 100.00% | 100.00% |

Notes:     * = Report on one polling center missing
           ** = Report on one constituency missing

Source: Supreme Elections Committee, Internal (Secret) Memo.

*Appendix XXVI*

# Terms of Reference

## Third Pre-Election Mission
## March 31 to April 7, 1993

MEMORANDUM

TO:        Members of the Pre-Election Mission

FROM:   Melissa A. Estok
            National Democratic Institute

DATE:    March 26, 1993

RE:        Terms of Reference

### Background

In anticipation of Yemen's first multiparty national elections, which are scheduled for April 27, 1993, NDI organized an initial pre-election assessment mission from January 26 to February.  During that mission, a group of Yemenis (including journalists, former government officials, academics and human rights activists) expressed interest in launching an independent movement to monitor the elections.  In late February, NDI Program Director Thomas O. Melia spent several days in Yemen discussing the possibility of implementing such an effort.  He met extensively with the interested group, now called the National Committee for Free Elections (NCFE), and with the body charged with supervising the elections, the Supreme Election Committee (SEC).  The outcome of these discussions was that indeed such a program could be organized.

In response to the NCFE's request for assistance, NDI organized a week of regional conferences, from March 8 to 15, for domestic election observers.  An additional conference was held in Sana'a for political parties that intend to train their own cadre of observers.  It was a successful program in which over 500 people participated.  Since then, the NCFE has begun to establish itself at the regional and local levels.  NDI will continue to support the efforts of the NCFE, and will keep a team in Yemen through the elections for that purpose.

## The Focus of this Assessment Mission

This mission has been organized in order to review the status of the electoral process just one month before the elections. Voter registration was completed one month ago, and the SEC is currently finalizing plans for the location and staffing of polling sites. Candidate registration is also about to begin. The purpose of our delegation is to gather information on the progress of the SEC in these areas, as well as about the general political situation to date.

As you know from our previous communication, during this week we intend also to focus on the role that women play in the electoral process. Since the beginning of NDI involvement in Yemen, we have noted the lack of visibility of women in political life. Through this mission, we hope to obtain concrete information regarding the participation of women in the process — their position in leadership, in political parties, in civic organizations and simply as registered voters. (An attached two-page summary describes our objectives for the mission in greater detail.)

## Methodology

Our principal method of arriving at determinations about the pre-election situation in Yemen will be to conduct interviews with a wide range of political contestants. In Sana'a, we will speak with government and election officials, candidates and civic leaders. We will also analyze the role of women in Yemeni political parties. Finally, we will interview leaders of independent organizations whose objectives relate to enhancing women's participation in civic and political life.

For most of our meetings, our entire delegation will be present. We will travel outside of Sana'a for two days, first to a village called Beni Hushais, a voting district where only two women registered to vote, and then to the city of Taiz, which had the highest percentage of female registrants outside of Sana'a. For most of our meetings, the entire delegation will be present. I expect there will be times, however, when it will be necessary to split up to conduct parallel meetings in order to cover as much ground as possible. Some meetings may be conducted through translators, while some Yemenis speak English.

### Additional Information

Two other Washington-based organizations have election-related programs in Yemen, and we will be hearing about them during our visit. The International Foundation for Electoral Systems (IFES) is providing administrative and technical assistance to the Supreme Election Commission. The International Republican Institute (IRI), which is affiliated to the U.S. Republican Party in the same way that NDI is affiliated informally to the Democratic Party, is preparing to send an international observer delegation to the elections. They will have a team in Sana'a during our week there, and we may hold several two-member meetings with them — or they may join us in certain meetings with election officials.

### Outcome of the Mission

Before we part at the end of the mission, our delegation will meet to discuss the content of a report, in order to ensure that your views are reflected. A draft report will then be prepared by my colleague from NDI, Palmer Kiperman, and myself, and will be sent to you for your comments before it is made public.

*Appendix XXVII*

# Delegation Schedule
## Third Pre-Election Mission
## March 31 to April 7, 1993

## Wednesday, March 31, 1993

| | |
|---|---|
| 10 am | Ahmed Abdul Rahman Qarhash, SEC Liaison with international organizations |
| 11 am | Amat Al-Alim Al-Soswa, Member of the PGC, Deputy Minister of Information |
| 12 noon | Ibtsam Al-Hammdi, Finance Director, National Committee for Free Elections |
| 1 pm | Abu Raas, Minister of Agriculture, SEC, Head of Technical Committee |
| | Fauzia Noman, Independent Candidate, former General Secretary of the Yemen Women's Union |
| 4 pm | Belgiza Al-Hadrani, Candidate, Al-Baath Party |
| 6 pm | National Committee for Free Elections |

## Thursday, April 1, 1993

| | |
|---|---|
| 11 am | Fatima Huraibi, Assistant to the President of the Agricultural Cooperative Union |
| 1 pm | Bedur Reimi, Member of the Al-Nasiri Party |
| | Hana Al-Habshi, Member of the Al-Nasiri Party |
| 3 pm | Abduraham Elmoassib, Director General, Environmental Health and the Ministry of Housing & Urban Planning |
| 5:30 pm | Ahlam Al-Mutawakkit, Radio Broadcaster, Member of the PGC |
| 7:30 pm | Hooria Almadhagi |

## Friday, April 2, 1993

Travel to Khowlan and Ibb — villages with no female registration
Travel to Taiz — a city with high female registration

## Saturday, April 3, 1993

Meet with Dr. Abdul Kadr Al-Junaid and teachers in Mohamed Ali-Oathman School

## Sunday, April 4, 1993

| | |
|---|---|
| 8:30 am | Mr. Abdulla Alakwaa, Member of the Al-Islah Party |
| 10 am | Aisha Abdul-Aziz, Member of the Yemeni Women's Union, Member of the YSP and currently works at the Ministry of Social Affairs |
| 1 pm | Mr. Jaralla Omar (YSP) |
| 4 pm | Dr. Raufa Hassan, Department of Communications, University of Sana'a, Deputy Chairwoman of the Yemen-American Friendship Association |
| 5:30 pm | Amat Al-Malek Zayid, Member of the Al-Haq party |

## Monday, April 5, 1993

| | |
|---|---|
| 10 am | Foreign Minister Abdul Karim Al-Eryani |
| 11:30 am | Raqia Homayden, SEC |
| 1 pm | Hafidh Fadel, SEC, Head of Legal Committee, SEC |
| 4 pm | Radilla Shamshir, Yemeni Women's Union |
| 5:30 pm | Anisa Raman and panel of journalists |

## Tuesday, April 6, 1993

NDI Delegation De-Briefing

*Appendix XXVIII*

# Interview Questions

## Third Pre-Election Mission
## March 31 to April 7, 1993

*Categories of Women Interviewed*

**I.  Civic Leaders**

1.  Yemeni Women's Union
2.  Society of Yemeni Women Voters
3.  National Committee for Free Elections

**II.  Formal Interviews for General Electoral Information**

1.  Government Officials
2.  Supreme Election Committee

**III.  Women Leaders in Government**

1.  Members of Parliament
2.  Deputy Minister of Information

**IV.  Women as Members of Political Parties**

1.  People's General Congress (PGC)
2.  Yemeni Socialist Party
3.  Al-Islah
4.  Sons of Yemen League

**V.  Women as Candidates in Upcoming National Legislative Elections**

1.  Independent Candidates
2.  Political Party Candidates
3.  PGC Candidates

**VI.  Women as Voters**

1.  Area of high female registration
2.  Area of low female registration

## I. General Questions

1. We all come to Yemen because of our interest in recent political liberalization begun in your country — Yemen has emerged as the country at the forefront in this region of the world in terms of democratic development. Compatibility of *sharia* and democracy...

2. How do you view the electoral process here to date? What are the successes? What are the problems?

3. Do you think the elections will change the lives of Yemenis? How? Will the effect differ between men and women?

4. Review registration statistics... The turnout of women, approximately 500,000, was seen by many as very high. What do you think about the figure? Why did some women register? Why did some women not register? Can you explain the disparity in registration participation from district to district?

5. Review number of women in leadership positions... What are the obstacles to women reaching positions of leadership in the government and other organizations?

6. What are your views on the current question of whether domestic and international observers should be permitted inside polling places on election day?

## II. Suggested Additional Questions for Category I

1. What are the general objectives of your organization?

2. Where do you receive funding?

3. What, if any, involvement have you had in the electoral process?

4. If you are involved in the electoral process, what difficulties did you encounter?

## III. Suggested Additional Questions for Category II

1. How do you view women's involvement within your organization? Have efforts been made to enhance women's participation in the elections?

2. (For SEC) What will be the system for women's polling stations? Will there be one for each male polling station, or, since fewer women registered, will there be fewer female polling stations?

3.  Do you anticipate any problems for women on election day?

4.  (For SEC) How did the system for encouraging women to register work? Would you make any changes in this system?

## IV.  Suggested Additional Questions for Category III

1.  Same as B

2.  How has your position, and that of women in general, changed since unification?

3.  What steps would you advise women to take who wish to seek electoral posts?

4.  What problems are there for women candidates?

## V.  Suggested Additional Questions for Category IV

1.  Same as B

2.  Same as B

3.  What steps do you advise women to take who wish to become politically active?

4.  What are the barriers that keep women from being politically active?

## VI.  Suggested Additional Questions for Category V

1.  What has been the reaction, public and private, to your candidacy?

2.  How have you financed your campaign? Does any official or private structure exist to support female candidates?

3.  Are there special concerns for women candidates? What are they?

## VII. Suggested Additional Questions for Category VI

1.  What were the demographics of women who registered? Age? Education? Political affiliation? Marital status? Class?

2.  Why did you register, or why not?

3.  If you registered, what will be the major deciding factors on how you will vote?

# National Democratic Institute
# for International Affairs

The National Democratic Institute for International Affairs (NDI) was established in 1983. By working with political parties and other institutions, NDI seeks to promote, maintain, and strengthen democratic institutions in new and emerging democracies. The Institute is headquartered in Washington, D.C. and has a staff of 120 with field offices in Africa, Asia, Eastern Europe, Latin America and the former Soviet Union.

NDI has conducted democratic development programs with more than 50 countries. Programs focus on six major areas:

*Political Party Training*: NDI conducts multipartisan training seminars in political development with a broad spectrum of democratic parties. NDI draws expert trainers from around the world to forums where members of fledgling parties learn first-hand the techniques of organization, communication and constituent contact.

*Election Processes*: NDI provides technical assistance for political parties and nonpartisan associations to conduct voter and civic education campaigns, and to organize election monitoring programs. The Institute has also organized more than 35 international observer delegations.

*Legislative Training*: NDI has organized legislative seminars focusing on legislative procedures, staffing, research information, constituent services and committee structures.

*Local Government*: Technical assistance on models of city management has been provided to national legislatures and municipal governments.

*Civil-Military Relations*: NDI brings together military and political leaders to promote dialogue and establish mechanisms for improving civil-military relations.

*Political and Civic Organization*: NDI supports and advises nonpartisan groups and political parties engaged in civic and voter education programs.

# National Democratic Institute for International Affairs

# Selected NDI Studies

- *The October 13, 1991 Legislative and Municipal Elections in Bulgaria*
- *The June 1990 Elections in Bulgaria*
- *An Assessment of the October 11, 1992 Election in Cameroon* (English and French)
- *Chile's Transition to Democracy, The 1988 Presidential Plebiscite* (English and Spanish)
- *Peaceful Transitions and the Cuban Democratic Platform: Report of an International Conference* (1991 English and Spanish)
- *1990 Elections in the Dominican Republic*
- *An Evaluation of the June 21, 1992 Elections in Ethiopia*
- *The November 1990 General Elections in Guatemala*
- *The New Democratic Frontier: A Country by Country Report on the Elections in Central and Eastern Europe* (English and Hungarian)
- *The 1990 General Elections in Haiti*
- *Nation Building: The U.N. and Namibia (1990)*
- *Coordinating Observers to the 1993 Elections in Niger* (English and French)
- *The October 1990 Elections in Pakistan*
- *The May 7, 1989 Panama Elections* (English and Spanish)
- *Voting for Greater Pluralism: The May 26, 1991 Elections in Paraguay*
- *Reforming the Philippine Electoral Process: 1986-1988* (Reissued Summer 1991)
- *The May 1990 Elections in Romania*
- *An Assessment of the Senegalese Electoral Code (1991)* (English and French)
- *Uneven Paths: Advancing Democracy in Southern Africa (1993)*
- *Strengthening Local Democracy in the Former Soviet Union: 1990-1992*
- *The October 31, 1991 National Elections in Zambia*